# What Is an Entrepreneur?

## David Robinson

**BOB ADAMS, INC.**
P U B L I S H E R S
Holbrook, Massachusetts

First published in Great Britain in 1990 by Kogan Page Limited, 120
Pentonville Road, London N1 9JN.

Published by Bob Adams, Inc., 260 Center Street, Holbrook,
Massachusetts, 02343.

This publication is designed to provide accurate and authoritative
information with regard to the subject matter covered. It is sold with
the understanding that the publisher is not engaged in rendering
legal, accounting, or other professional advice. If legal advice or
other expert assistance is required, the services of a competent
professional person should be sought.

Manufactured in the United States of America.

A   B   C   D   E   F   G   H   I   J

ISBN: 1-55850-055-3

# Acknowledgments

I am very grateful to numerous clients, friends, and colleagues who have contributed in different ways to the material which I used in writing this book. I particularly wish to acknowledge the help of Professor Michael Earle for allowing me access to the library of Templeton College, Oxford, to the staff of the Information Department of Spicer & Oppenheim and to a number of secretaries at my firm who worked tirelessly on the preparation of the text.

# Contents

**Chapter 1**

Introduction to the Entrepreneur .......................... 9
A matter of definition. Born or made? How
entrepreneurial are you?

**Chapter 2**

Innovator ......................................... 17
Brainwaves and cheap copies. Looking for the
incongruous. How it's done. Tunnel vision. The thrill
of the chase. Super salesman. Visionary or profiteer?

**Chapter 3**

Risk-taker ......................................... 29
The competitive urge. Failure—who cares! Breaking
the rules. Concert parties. The wild ones. A feeling of
unimportance? Knowing the odds.

**Chapter 4**

Individualist .................................... .......... 49
The rebellious urge. Who can you trust? Non-team
playing. The making of a team-player. I know best!

**Chapter 5**

Manager ......................................... 65
Opportunist or planner? Typical watershed decision
points. Retaining the good qualities. Non-planning. A
sound judge of people. A healthy team. The ethics of
management. Unsafe assumptions. Older and wiser?

## Chapter 6

Prima Donna ........................................ 83
The Napoleon factor. An impossible partner? Follow
my leader. A team of heroes. Living with a whirlwind.
24 hours a day. Money and power. Family man. Private
lives. Keeping it in the family.

## Chapter 7

Summing Up ....................................... 105
Alike or different? Developing entrepreneurial
capacity. Golden rules for the entrepreneur. The naked
entrepreneur.

Bibliography ........................................ 111

Index ............................................... 115

*Chapter 1*

# Introduction to the Entrepreneur

## A matter of definition

If you are walking down a street with a friend and he points to someone and says, "That's John—he's an entrepreneur," what sort of person do you imagine? Is John the local bingo hall baron or property magnate? Is he a bond dealer or the owner of the video store downtown? Does he drive a Porsche and have a villa in Portugal, or have two children at private school and life membership at the local golf club?

Any or all of these descriptions could be true. The word "entrepreneur" is increasing in everyday use in the vocabulary of our enterprise society. Literally, it means someone who "carries something between" two parties—in other words a middleman. But an entrepreneur is not an altruistic or disinterested party: quite the contrary, he is distinctly interested in profit and wealth creation.

Middlemen come in all shapes and sizes but the implicit assumption is that they actually do little real work. The middleman is thought of as a "smart aleck" who makes a profit at the expense of two less bright colleagues. By this definition, the entrepreneur would do little to create wealth—just siphon off some for himself. However, this is far from real life observation of the entrepreneur.

Few entrepreneurs, if any, could be described in these crude and simplistic terms. The character we are seeking to define is much more complex and elusive than this literal extension of the word would suggest. More recognizable, perhaps, is the picture of the entrepreneur as "super hero"—the wealthy, larger-than-life risk-taker and business autocrat. He may be tinged with megalomania, and his activities admired and written about alongside of pop stars and politicians. Living in a world apart from ordinary mortals, such people seem to have the power to change the destinies not only of companies but of whole industries.

This archetype, too, is inadequate. There are very few who fit this mold and they are scarcely representative of what is acknowledged as a large and growing group of people.

For the purposes of this book, we need a recognizable set of assumptions about the sort of person we are examining. No definition can be either comprehensive or wholly satisfactory: all that can be aimed for is a sufficiently wide scope for *most* of the target group to be included.

We shall assume that our "entrepreneur" is:

- Involved in what may generally be described as "business," whether making, selling or trading in things.

- The sole proprietor of his or her enterprise—although, as we shall discuss later, entrepreneurial partnerships offer an interesting exception to this assumption.

- Established in the sense of having satisfied his immediate material needs but remaining ambitious to grow in influence and wealth.

These assumptions describe entrepreneurs in terms of what they do and how they do it.

An alternative description can be based not on what they *do* but on what they *are*. The contention of this book is that you can just as certainly recognize an entrepreneur from the way he or she thinks and behaves as from whether he has made a million or ten million dollars. It argues that within a broad section of people drawn from widely differing backgrounds, cultures, and intellectual groups, some key traits are commonly discernible. Many years' experience suggest that they occur with sufficient frequency to offer some general insights which may prove useful both to the independent observer and to the entrepreneur himself. (For simplicity, the personal pronoun "he" is used through the text to include both males and females.)

Our aim is to strip away the hyperbole and self-promotion and explore the characteristics that go into the make-up of the entrepreneur, relying on: the findings of academics; the revelations of individuals in their more unguarded and frank moments of self-analysis; but, most of all, on 25 years' experience of close personal and working relationships with entrepreneurs—both the successful and the failures. Observing the "naked" entrepreneur is an instructive process. It will help us to understand some of those inner motives that contribute to the energy and commitment that single out the entrepreneur from his fellow men. It will help us to recognize the early indications of entrepreneurial capacity and to encourage and nurture them. It will also warn us of the dangers of making invalid assumptions about how such individuals are likely to behave in particular circumstances. Most of all, it aims to offer some new insight into the behavior of a group of people whose activities are of fundamental importance to the growth of any free enterprise economy.

In summary, then, an entrepreneur, whether male or female, has already chosen a way of life dedicated to the pursuit of money and power, has demonstrated some success in that pursuit and shown business associates, staff, friends and family those qualities (both endearing and less so!) which have contributed to that success.

## Born or made?

The point of departure on our journey of exploration must be to seek some answer to the question of whether the entrepreneur springs from the cradle with all his faculties, drives, and traits preformed, needing only the opportunity to exploit them later in some suitable business environment; or whether the entrepreneurial character is formed by a process of "conditioning," by a combination of circumstances and the example (and influence) of others.

This question is important for a number of reasons. If entrepreneurs are "born," then once we can identify and understand the main distinguishing characteristics, there is little point in those lacking them to attempt to embark on such a path: the likelihood of failure would be too great. Equally, those responsible for developing an individual's talents, whether school teachers, trainers, or business superiors, would be advised to concentrate on more useful skills than encouraging independent enterprise. If it was certain that these distinguishing features were "born" into individuals, this would equally suggest that talent spotting for the budding entrepreneur would, indeed, start in the school playground.

Conversely, proof of the proposition that entrepreneurs are "made" by their experiences and working environment would encourage the creation of such conditions, particularly within established businesses. Many companies have attempted to establish a "nursery" for budding entrepreneurs—generally, it must be said, with poor results.

The answer to this question lies in what John G. Burch, writing in the September-October 1986 edition of *Business Horizons* calls "the galaxy of personality traits (which) characterize individuals who have a propensity to behave entrepreneurially." He lists nine as being "more salient." These are:

1. *A desire to achieve.* Most entrepreneurs push to conquer problems and give birth to a successful venture.
2. *Hard work.* Most entrepreneurs are workaholics (in many instances they have to be in order to achieve their goals).
3. *Nurturing quality.* They take charge of and watch over a venture until it can stand alone.
4. *Acceptance of responsibility.* They are morally, legally, and mentally accountable for their ventures.
5. *Reward orientation.* They want to achieve, work hard, and take responsibility, but they also want to be rewarded handsomely for their efforts—and rewards can come in forms other than money, such as recognition and respect.
6. *Optimism.* They live by the philosophy that this is the best of times and that anything is possible.
7. *Orientation to excellence.* They often desire to achieve something outstanding that they can be proud of—something first class.
8. *Organization.* Most are good at bringing together the components of a venture—they are wholly "take charge" people.
9. *Profit orientation.* They want to make a profit, but the profit serves primarily as a meter to gauge their degree of achievement and performance.

Of these traits, two stand out as being more likely to be "inborn" qualities than the others—the desire to achieve and the capacity for hard work. Several research studies have shown that entrepreneurs are convinced that they can command their own destinies. In the jargon of the behavioral scientist, the "locus of control" of the entrepreneur lies within himself rather than the world about him. He believes that his destiny lies in his own hands rather than as a consequence of the actions of others. While this is also a fairly common characteristic of successful leaders, whether in business or not, it exists in such a sharply emphasized form in the entrepreneur that it can verge on the obsessive. It is this self-belief which stimulates him to act in a highly individualistic and often rebellious way. It creates an attitude which accepts amounts of work which would be quite unacceptable to ordinary mortals, encourages persistence long after others have given up and underpins a reputation for unswerving dedication to a concept, product or business initiative.

The capacity to work exceptionally hard (and long) in pursuit of a particular project requires a combination of physical, emotional, and intellectual energy which cannot be artificially stimulated—except in short bursts. We are all familiar with the adrenaline surge which accompanies the achievement of an exceptional task. Feats of endurance and resilience are almost as commonplace on the battlefields of commerce as they are in those real wars. The extraordinary facility of the entrepreneur is to sustain that same commitment and capacity *in the long term*. Entrepreneurs claim that the "work" involved is almost wholly pleasurable and that their unstinting commitment to it is therefore no more than self-indulgence. This may be true from their point of view. Those working with the entrepreneur, exhausted from trying to keep pace with the unbounding energy he shows, would equally argue that the effort involved is "work" of a very demanding order. They would leave us in no doubt that this characteristic is both exceptional and rare.

While a facility to organize, to understand and manage risk, and to be strongly motivated by personal gain, can be developed in individuals in the appropriate environment, it seems that these two basic character traits must be inborn if the entrepreneur is to succeed. Writing about their early lives (normally with an eye to making the best of the story), many successful businessmen reflect on how they exploited their first opportunity. It seldom seems to have been either an easy or an uncomplicated breakthrough. In every case, there was a moment of truth—a point of decision when a "safe" option was rejected and a risk undertaken. Was it a calm, cold and rational decision or impulsive and intuitive? Whatever intellectual processes were at work, it seems certain that the "demon" driving the entrepreneur took hold at that moment and a career was launched.

## How entrepreneurial are you?

John Burch offers a further insight into the "tendencies" which indicate how entrepreneurial (on non-entrepreneurial) individuals are likely to be. His matrix is reproduced on the following page.

At the "non-entrepreneurial" end of each axis is the person least likely to take that role—in Mr. Burch's analysis, a laborer. At the other end is the person most likely to take that role—what he calls the "inventrepreneur"—who not only exploits an idea, but invents it in the first place. Between these two extremes, he shows examples of the types of job people may have, corresponding to the "tendencies" they show.

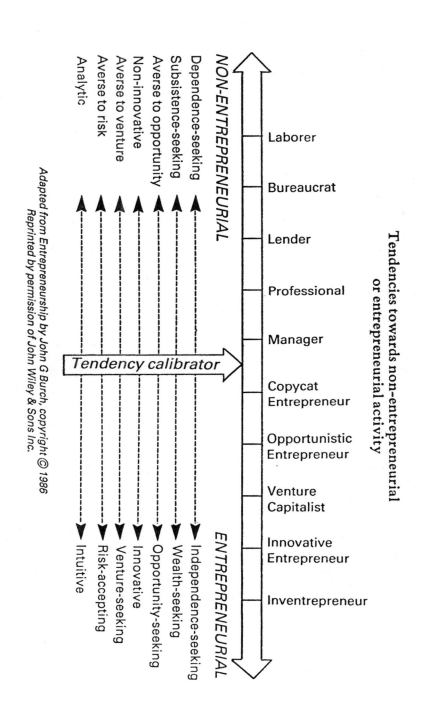

**NON-ENTREPRENEURIAL**

Dependence-seeking
Subsistence-seeking
Averse to opportunity
Non-innovative
Averse to venture
Averse to risk
Analytic

**Tendency calibrator**

**ENTREPRENEURIAL**

Independence-seeking
Wealth-seeking
Opportunity-seeking
Innovative
Venture-seeking
Risk-accepting
Intuitive

Laborer

Bureaucrat

Lender

Professional

Manager

Copycat Entrepreneur

Opportunistic Entrepreneur

Venture Capitalist

Innovative Entrepreneur

Inventrepreneur

Tendencies towards non-entrepreneurial or entrepreneurial activity

Adapted from Entrepreneurship by John G Burch, copyright © 1986
Reprinted by permission of John Wiley & Sons Inc.

In common with most models, this matrix contains elements of both simplification and generalization. Although it should, for this reason, be approached with some caution, it does offer an interesting, if rather rudimentary, basis for self-assessment. If your personal behavior is firmly at the right-hand end of the scale for *all elements*, you have the makings of an entrepreneur. If any veer to the left of the center line, however marginally, think again.

## A structured approach
Research into entrepreneurial behavior is concentrated on three, archetypal roles:

- Innovator.
- Risk-taker.
- Manager.

The successful individual must simultaneously perform well in each role; it is no use, for example, having a marvellous idea and risking all your resources on it only to fail miserably in its practical delivery.

This broad structure is followed in the book but amplified in several significant ways. The conventional analysis offers important insights into such people's business approach and behavior and, indeed, individual chapters are devoted to each of the above headings. However, that is only part of the story. The missing elements relate to what such people are actually *like* as commercial colleagues, as bosses, as business associates, or as husbands, wives, or fathers. Our investigation of the "naked" entrepreneur has, therefore, two additional, and crucial facets: the entrepreneur as *individualist* and as *prima donna*.

In chapters devoted to these topics, we explore the characteristics that make such people "different" and how they can be uncomfortable, demanding, but inspiring colleagues. Anyone with experience in dealing with entrepreneurs will testify to the importance of understanding the "chemistry" involved. In these chapters, the test tube and microscope are brought into play.

Throughout the text, case studies and examples are used to highlight particular points. They are drawn from personal experience and therefore reflect "real life." None, however, is exactly identifiable with any individual or company but they are rather composites based on a number of cases. Any comments, whether critical or complimentary, should therefore not be assumed to apply personally to any of the many entrepreneurs with whom the author has had the privilege and pleasure of working over many years.

*Chapter 2*

# Innovator

Every new business has some element of innovation within it. Opening a new restaurant, starting a garden center or a pet shop, is innovative as far as the owners are concerned. They are taking business risks and they may well see themselves as being entrepreneurs. It is quite probable, however, that the new venture has little real novelty beyond the location involved and the commendable initiative being taken by the proprietors. True innovation occurs when the venture, product or idea has a striking degree of difference from what has gone before. The change itself might be small: what matters is the extent to which it represents a genuinely new way of doing things.

Take, for example, the case of the McDonald's hamburger chain. Hamburger stores were commonplace when that company first entered the marketplace. They could easily have chosen to adopt a similar formula to their competitors' by offering cheap, no frills, fast food, with success depending on price and location and little else. The management of McDonald's, however, realized that customers would pay a premium price for their hamburger if it was served cheerfully and efficiently, in clean and well-organized outlets to a consistently high quality wherever the consumer saw the McDonald's sign. The innovation involved was therefore not about changing the product but about developing a replicable presentation formula which has now conquered the world. It is this element of insight and novelty that distinguishes the entrepreneurial approach from that of the simple copies.

Peter Drucker, in his book *Innovation and Entrepreneurship*, has described this process of successful innovation as being "the specific instrument of entrepreneurship." In examining the characteristics of the entrepreneur, we must explore both the source of this innovative urge and how it is realized in practice.

## Brainwaves and cheap copies

It is easy to confuse innovation with invention. It is often assumed that the innovator is a wild-eyed scientist working at his laboratory bench late into the night to develop some miracle product which will revolutionize our daily lives. Undoubtedly, there are such brilliant individuals who have a genius for finding some previously unthought of solution to a problem, a totally new material or process, or new products that will fundamentally change the way people work or spend their leisure. There is a seemingly endless catalog of inventive geniuses who have made historic breakthroughs in a whole range of scientific and technological fields: Alexander Graham Bell, Thomas Edison, and Marie Curie are just a few of the names that spring to mind. Given their genius for invention it is perhaps surprising to note how few of these illustrious people were ultimately successful as entrepreneurs.

It is equally true that "invention" in terms of new products and processes is as often as not the result of a team effort involving a number of individuals working over a long period within either an academic institution or a large company—environments not normally associated with entrepreneurialism. The results of their work are, however, often associated with later and highly successful entrepreneurial development, while the individuals in the research team—the true inventors—are seldom direct participants in this second stage.

In the classical sense of being inventors, therefore, it is unwise to assume that entrepreneurs either inevitably need that capability or that those who possess it can complement their inventiveness with the ability to exploit their ideas. Innovation is essentially a creative process, but not necessarily one which involves novel products or services. Indeed, it is quite likely that the entrepreneur himself is not a particularly creative person in the conventional meaning of that word.

What are the issues which condition the entrepreneur's ability to innovate and where can we draw the line between the brainwave and the cheap copy?

## Looking for the incongruous

Experience suggests that the entrepreneur often has a move vivid and active imagination than his colleagues. He foresees business opportunities in a more realistic and complete form and the consequences of actions which he can take with greater clarity than his peers. Take, for example, the case of the promoter of the hula hoop. There must have been some point at which the person concerned imagined boys and girls on street corners playing with a ring of plastic in a way that was completely novel at the time. His vision must have been sufficiently strong to encourage him to develop and market the product. There are doubtless many similar examples. But what led to that vision in the first place?

The explanation is that entrepreneurs have a restless interest in the incongruous. An incongruity is something which seems to the entrepreneur to be not quite "right." It is rather like a flaw that is found by an expert in a fine work of art which is not apparent to the layman. Once he has spotted it, the entrepreneur is not satisfied until he has found a way of making the incongruous "right" again. For example, he might worry over the proposition, "Surely there ought to be more for young people to do in this town than go to the movies" or the problem of, "How do I keep my chrysanthemums from blowing over when it's windy?" His imagination sets to work and his profit motivation is stimulated. Whether they are aware of it or not, entrepreneurs habitually collect information about their environment and review it for such incongruous features. The reason they do this is that incongruous situations offer opportunities for exploitation.

Typically, an incongruity will fall into one of several generic categories:

1. A mismatch between the way something is currently done and how it could be done more effectively using a radically different approach.
2. A poorly satisfied user demand that can be better met by a new product or service.
3. An opportunity for a new venture arising out of some change in the economic, legal or business climate.
4. A recognition of an incipient user demand resulting from the creative application of some new technology.

These four categories will be illustrated from common experience of successful entrepreneurial ventures.

### Doing things better

It was not many years ago that the idea of the supermarket was born. Previously, groceries had been sold in small specialist shops on main streets and street corners. The entrepreneurial opportunity was recognized when the concept of self-service was born. Wage costs formed the dominant part of the overheads of retailers and the breakthrough came from examining ways of employing labor more efficiently and using the savings made to set cheaper prices. Traditionally, the "assistant" had been the servant of the customer, offering advice, explaining the merits of the product, weighing, slicing or counting it, packing and pricing it. The innovation was to stand this idea on its head. Well-presented, prepacked, and prepriced products do not need sales assistants. The customer "serves" the shop assistant on the till who must simply total the bill and collect the money. This development led logically to an expansion in store sizes, introduction of the "own label" concept, and the purchasing domination of the major grocery chains. In origin, however, the entrepreneurial idea was simple—"Let the customer select the product himself and thereby save us labor costs so that we can reduce the price of the article."

## The better mousetrap

It is often said that the world would beat a path to the door of the man who invented a "better mousetrap." Identifying a conventional process or product and being convinced that it can be carried out or made more efficiently and economically required, in itself, a leap of the imagination. To follow it through to a successful exploitation required additional qualities of a quite exceptional order.

Before the introduction of Letraset in 1960, printers and designers used costly and time-consuming methods of hand drawing or cutting out and pasting down type pulls to make up artwork for advertisements, leaflets and the like. "What if," speculated Dai Davies, the inventor of the system, "the old-fashioned child's transfer that you soak in a saucer of water and slide off, could be used for lettering?" At the time, most people regarded such a process as impracticable and Dai had few supporters in his pioneering work. Despite this skepticism, shortages of funds and many setbacks, he showed remarkable dedication to his pursuit of this apparently simple concept. He was convinced that the printing industry was ready for this "better mousetrap" and after four years of struggle was able to launch his new product.

The market proved not only receptive to the new idea but willing to pay a price sufficient to sustain the growth of the Letraset company over a number of years. It experienced quite a remarkable success and traditional methods were soon superseded throughout the western world.

The introduction, and increasingly widespread us, of desktop publishing has overtaken many of the applications for Letraset. However, the story of the development of this product, from invention to

20

commercial exploitation, offers a vivid example of the way in which conventional thinking can be challenged by the determined entrepreneur.

## A change in the climate
The digging of the Suez canal (completed in 1869) had a dramatic effect on the world shipping industry. The distance saved by using the canal instead of the Cape of Good Hope route on a voyage between northern France or England and Bombay is 4,000 miles, and the canal offers the shortest route between the eastern seaboard of North America and the port of the Indian Ocean. It was clear from the earliest inception of the project that the canal would have a fundamental effect on the structure and economics of world trade. It was only those more entrepreneurial ship-owning companies who fully realized this potential and organized both fleets and cargoes to take full advantage of it.

A more up-to-date example will be the consequences of the Channel Tunnel between England and France and the opportunities such a structural change will offer those who can clearly envisage the consequential changes in the patterns of business operations.

## Creating a new demand
The invention of television is a classic example of a product being created to meek a market need no one previously realized existed. John Logie Baird saw the potential value of transmitting live pictures into people's homes. He saw it as filling a gap in the available forms of communication rather than offering a reaction to a well-articulated public demand. There are many examples of such breakthrough products. The Sony Walkman, the digital watch, and the portable computer were all developed on this basis.

## How it's done
The entrepreneur sees opportunities to innovate in terms of their potential to make money for him. The process of spotting the incongruities and the opportunities they create varies enormously from one individual to another. For some it is a systematic and painstaking process, carefully documented. For others it is more inspirational and spasmodic. However, all entrepreneurs appear to share the common characteristic of being extremely sensitive to the world about them and particularly capable of creating an "internal" vision of how it might change if the entrepreneurial idea was pursued to its full extent. In this process there is clearly a role for inspirational brainwaves. Cheap

copies, on the other hand, rarely if ever represent genuinely entrepreneurial opportunities.

The entrepreneur is someone who has the insight to spot a business opportunity that has novelty and is innovative. What happens next? Many people have good business ideas, spot the opportunities, see the exploitation potential, but do nothing about it. In the case of the entrepreneur, certain special characteristics start to take over, and he typically adopts quite a different approach from the rest of us.

## Tunnel vision

The words "obsessive" or "fixated" are sometimes used to describe the entrepreneurial drive. It is certainly true that many entrepreneurs become so committed to a particular concept or product that in its pursuit their behavior becomes unconventional, even outlandish. There is a fine line between the behavior of the dedicated enthusiast and that of the irrational bigot. Successful entrepreneurs avoid being caught in this trap because they know that their success depends on the support and influence of others who are not impressed by extremism. However, they are usually as dedicated to and protective of their idea as any parent defending a child.

The entrepreneur's commitment to his idea is obviously stimulated, at least in part, by self-interest, whether measured in terms of financial reward or person recognition. The more intriguing element is the almost missionary zeal with which an apparently trivial innovation is pursued. It seems that this stems typically from the entrepreneur's strong sense of independence and a recurring need to demonstrate it through succeeding by his own efforts. A darker interpretation is that this only reflects the entrepreneur's essential insecurity in the face of the world about him and his need to perform exceptionally to leave some sort of mark on it.

Whatever the deeper motives, it is quite clear that the entrepreneur has an astonishing capacity to be dedicated to the idea or product he is promoting. This shows itself in the tenacity with which he will endure setbacks and failures in the pursuit of his goal, without any apparent loss of enthusiasm or confidence. He does not see this as in any way irrational, but rather accepts that the process of convincing those around him of his own view is more lengthy and troublesome than it should be. Sometimes his patience runs out and persistence turns to irritation. "Why can't you see it my way?" he may thunder. The fact of the matter is that what is self-evident to him is rarely so obvious to others, who are more concerned with why something *won't* work than why it *will*. Tunnel vision has its advantages—and its drawbacks too.

## The thrill of the chase

Entrepreneurs with the capacity to pursue their ideas with unremitting vigor and enthusiasm also have a novel source of personal motivation: that is, the pure enjoyment many obtain from the process of convincing others of the rightness of their own view. We shall examine later the question of the entrepreneur's view of risk taking but whatever the potential rewards, few ventures can succeed without the active support and collaboration of suppliers, customers, bankers, and so on.

The process of persuading someone to buy the product, finance the volume or share the risk can be likened to "the chase." The target is stalked, cornered, and bagged. The sight of an entrepreneur returning from a foray in the world of finance, having newly converted a doubting banker to his cause, is quite remarkable. The nearest comparable analogy is that of the missionary having newly converted a heathen to the true faith!

A crucial part of this whole process is, of course, the effective communication of the entrepreneur's idea to the people he needs to convince in order to bring it to fruition. This requires salesmanship.

## Super salesman

All the available evidence suggests that entrepreneurs come from a wide variety of psychological types, ranging from intuitive extroverts to thinking introverts. To be successful, however, they must share a capability to persuade. When the product or service is itself innovative, the process of persuasion involves a high degree of effective salesmanship.

Some key elements seem to be common to the process and the approach used by successful entrepreneurs. These are:

- A thoroughly researched prospectus.
- An understanding of buying behavior.
- An ability to present clearly and succinctly.

### A clear prospectus

In working through a new idea the successful entrepreneur develops his prospectus in a great degree of detail. Although it is not often written down in such detail, he examines every angle using what might most conveniently be called a "role-playing" approach. He imagines how he would behave if he were a customer using the new product, what would be involved if he were making it, supplying the raw materials, working in the factory or providing the finance. He imagines what role he, the entrepreneur, would be playing and how he would promote and develop the idea in the marketplace. He looks for flaws and difficulties in the argument and although these may never be publicly aired, agonizes over the risks of failure and disappointment.

The result of this process is a very complete picture of the project he wishes to promote. It may take weeks or months to complete: despite their reputation for instant action, successful entrepreneurs rarely rush into new situations. Any major decision is only taken after completing this very detailed and exhaustive analysis process. When influencing others there is always a need for well-documented project information, but this seldom represents more than the tip of the iceberg of this thinking process.

### Understanding buying behavior
Armed with a detailed knowledge of his project, the entrepreneur next assesses the individual interests of the parties that he wants to persuade. When looking at the project from the standpoint of these other people, the key question is, "What is in it for me?"

Consider, for example, the case of an entrepreneur whose project is to persuade a large library to allow him to take facsimile copies of all their rare books, store them on optical disk and sell the rights of access to this data to academic institutions and publishers. He needs to raise capital for the venture and persuade both the suppliers of the information, namely the library, and the prospective users, that it will be of benefit to them. He must first imagine himself as the chief librarian, custodian of a public institution, deeply conscious of his stewardship responsibilities for a public asset. In dealing with academics and publishing houses he must understand how they are likely to view such an information source, how important it might be to them, and how much they would be prepared to pay for it. Last but not least, he must consider the position of the financier and whether this venture is likely to be interesting from the point of long-term capital gain. He will need to meet all parties during the process of putting his project together and deal appropriately with their concerns and interests. The techniques used in each case would be different: some would be interested in the technology and the status they might gain by being associated with such a venture; others might see an immediate cost advantage or a way of taking an initiative ahead of their competitors. In any event the entrepreneur must understand the likely buying behavior of each of his essential collaborators.

In this example, the collaborators are as much buying an idea as a physical product whose characteristics can be easily demonstrated. Selling ideas requires quite different techniques and the really persuasive entrepreneur is able to convey not only a very tangible picture of how his operation would work, but also a strongly convincing message about the benefits that would flow to the particular party he is addressing.

This chameleon-like capability to change the whole style and nature of the approach is one of the characteristics enjoyed by many successful entrepreneurs. It extends to the way they use language, gesture, and analogy, and remind the listener of previous experience. Taken together, the ability to make a direct appeal in a clear and unequivocal way to the subconscious interest of the "buyer" is a vital skill possessed by many who are successful in promoting new venture.

**The power to communicate**

The communication techniques used by entrepreneurs are many and varied. They are, however, usually more powerful oral than written communicators and the language they employ is often very simple and direct. They tend to make extensive use of analogy and have the skill to present a complex idea in a straightforward and vivid form. Entrepreneurs seem to draw many of these analogies from childhood and sporting situations. This perhaps reveals a deeper belief that business or enterprise is, itself, a form of sporting activity. They often talk rapidly, using very short and powerful sentences to illustrate an idea. Since optimism is a general characteristic of entrepreneurs, their methods of communication tend to underline this feature.

For example, they often prefer to walk and talk rather than sit quietly behind a desk. Their concentration on the issue in hand is so intense that major distractions, such as loudly ringing telephones or the hubbub of a factory floor, go wholly unnoticed.

When presenting ideas and persuading others, entrepreneurs tend to be better talkers than listeners. Their attention span is often relatively short and they have a tendency to interrupt before other have completed a sentence. Some entrepreneurs use colorful language; few are dry and academic. Hearing an entrepreneur in full flow, selling a new venture to a potential collaborator, is a fascinating and enjoyable experience. It is a brave man, however, who attempts to stand in the path of the verbal bulldozer!

## Visionary or profiteer?

The entrepreneur has to be innovative, committed, persistent and persuasive. But what's in it for him? Crude analysis would suggest that there is one simple, overriding and all-persuasive motive—the pursuit of money. But his analysis is inevitably simplistic and the available academic research demonstrates that, although the pursuit of wealth is a powerful influence in the early stages of an entrepreneur's career, its power rapidly diminishes above a certain threshold of achievement. Despite this, the entrepreneur is driven on to greater and greater effort in terms of the energy and commitment which he brings to his role. This "demon," which appears to stimulate an exceptional response well beyond the stage at which most would be wholly satisfied with their life's work, is worthy of closer analysis.

The following simple and general categorization of entrepreneurs seems to fit common experience:

- Visionaries.
- Strivers.
- Dealers.


### Visionaries

The visionary entrepreneur is spurred on by a general dissatisfaction with the way things are in the world. This is not to suggest that he is a social improver; rather he has a restless conviction that the untidy ends of the world around him can and should be tied up. In search of a better product or service, many concerned with technological innovation have a deep-seated conviction that the way things are done now is less than satisfactory. They search for better materials, improved processes, more effective products for the consumer or the industrialist. They appear to have a fairly deep conviction that the world should be an ordered and efficient place, and their products and ideas are based on this assumption. In many entrepreneurial initiatives in the service sector the new idea eliminates some previously inefficient part of the system. To be a visionary does not, of course, exclude a genuine desire for profit and capital. Its power as a motivating force, however, persists well beyond the first million dollars, and it appears that those endowed with this quality never lose it. The visionary is the most likely of all entrepreneurial types to be a genuine innovator.

## Strivers

Although entrepreneurs are commonly expected to be confident and extroverted, the truth is that many feel both deeply insecure in their relationship with society and a continuing need to prove their capacity to be successful. This is less a case of inadequacy of character than a deep distrust of the permanence of their own achievements. It is curious that the more wealthy and successful some entrepreneurs appear to be, the more paranoid they become about the risk of failure. Even those who achieve secure fortunes far in excess of what they would ever need for total comfort in old age are driven to pile yet more on to their list of achievements and capital.

Such people never seem to be satisfied with what they have achieved. They push themselves relentlessly forward and must always have at least one, and preferably several, new initiatives under way at one time. They are constantly "striving" for something increasingly difficult to determine. They are fiercely competitive and consequently often make poor company when relaxed enjoyment should take precedence over "winning." They are exhausting companions, never off duty and always probing and testing new ideas and theories. Generally, they do not seem to be very happy people: they lack the capacity to relax sufficiently deeply or long enough to benefit from the more enduring human pleasures. The type of venture in which the striving entrepreneur engages is less important to him than the fact of being involved in enterprising ventures. In the extreme, anything will do, and such individuals often prefer pure gambling to inactivity.

Strivers, like visionaries, have a restless view of the world. Their interests are likely to be more eclectic in their pursuit of new projects, more obviously driven by their own self-interest. It is from this group of entrepreneurs that the caricature of the distrusting, miserly, and egocentric multi-millionaire is drawn.

## Dealers

This group is the mist dispassionate and calculating of the three. The dealer will look for an opportunity in any marketplace, in any country, or in any commodity. He sees his skills as those of being able to act more cleverly, more quickly or more powerfully than his competitors. Typical of this category are entrepreneurs who spot a shortage in one market and an available supply in another, who see unrealized potential in property or who can bring together two parties with a mutual interest. As well as being highly streetwise, they also can be extremely inventive and are often very able judges of people. The financial motive tends to be extremely strong with dealers but once mastered it is often the pleasure of the dealing process that rewards the entrepreneur rather than the financial gain alone. Many very prominent international entrepreneurs show these characteristics very clearly: their company portfolio-building and their aggressive takeover tactics are indicators of this basic approach.

It is worth noting that these categories do not include either gamblers or what might otherwise appear to be normal, level-headed, and sensible people. The reason for the exclusion of gamblers is that successful entrepreneurs are seldom, if ever, serious gamblers. We shall examine this question in more depth in the next chapter.

It is perhaps more difficult to answer the question why the categories do not include the normal and level-headed individuals. It would be foolish to deny that many who have developed ideas, exploited them and made fortunes either alone or with teams of colleagues appear to be anything other than normal and level-headed. It can be argued, however, that these apparently calm exteriors conceal powerful internal motivational forces which single out those who genuinely succeed and those who fail. Achievement must, of course, be measured against ambition. The will to make an adequate living through an enterprising venture is wholly commendable. The entrepreneur goes well beyond this modest initial goal and the driving force is powerful and long term.

## Summary
Above all, the entrepreneur achieves success through innovation. He looks for the incongruous in the world, treats it as an opportunity and then subjects his vision to detailed and thorough scrutiny. His commitment is coupled with an ability to see the project from the point of view of others and to identify their self-interest during the selling process. Powerful methods of communication are commonplace among successful entrepreneurs who have many of the skills of the effective salesman. They are driven by a wide variety of influence, not least that of the creation of personal wealth. Those who succeed in the long term, however, are subject to complex motivating forces.

*Chapter 3*

# Risk-taker

All entrepreneurs love to compete. The essence of any competition is that the outcome is uncertain. Hence there is an element of risk, and it is the characteristic of the entrepreneur as a risk-taker which we examine in this chapter.

## The competitive urge

The bulk of academic research to date confirms the observation that entrepreneurs are abnormally (and sometimes excessively) competitive people. This is often as much apparent in their private lives as in their business activities. For example, anyone who has played golf or tennis against a successful entrepreneur will testify to the aggression such people bring to their game. Even minor domestic issues are often tinged with the feeling that the entrepreneur not only needs to "score points," but always wants to have the last word (the personal pronoun "I" is seldom underused.) There are even situations in which the entrepreneur appears to be competing with himself.

Some already very successful businessmen set themselves what appear to outsiders to be unnecessarily punishing targets. This behavior can reach extraordinary if not bizarre lengths. In one case, an entrepreneur made promises to his bankers about the outcome of a merger which seemed so extravagant that the deal almost floundered on the spot. He set himself a most daunting task and it required all his energy and ingenuity to complete it. That fact that he did so meant he ultimately won approval and applause from all involved. The more perplexing question is, why he did it in the first place.

In a famous article in the *Harvard Business Review* ("The Dark Side of Entrepreneurship," November-December 1985), Manfred Kets de

Vries argues that the entrepreneur is constantly in search of a way of controlling his environment. Some entrepreneurs, says de Vries, "are strikingly ambivalent when an issue of control surfaces—they are filled with fantasies of grandiosity, influence, power, and authority, yet also feel helpless. They seem to fear that their grandiose desires will get out of control and place them ultimately at the mercy of others." Winning any competition, however insignificant it may appear, puts the entrepreneur in control of the situation. The scale of the competition, the risks involved, and the nature of the prize are less relevant than the driving urge to compete. Taking de Vries's analysis a stage further, entrepreneurs can be seen as deeply insecure individuals with a recurring need to prove themselves to the world around them.

An alternative explanation is more straightforward—namely that entrepreneurs feel naturally superior as individuals and seek every opportunity to prove it. Doubtless, entrepreneurs have a great degree of self-belief and commitment and these qualities are an essential part of their make-up. However, a feeling of natural superiority does not in itself account for the extraordinary lengths to which many successful men and women will go to win at all costs. The much publicized confrontations between highly successful international businessmen seem to be out of keeping with the image of the relaxed, confident and self-assured entrepreneur. It is no coincidence that these people also choose to compete in such fields of sport (the more expensive the better) as yachting, power boat racing and horse racing. An element of irrationality and personal vendetta sometimes surfaces, doubtless to the concern and discomfiture of the work colleagues: it seems that scores have to be settled almost irrespective of cost and potential benefit.

Undoubtedly, it is the almost obsessive concern for competition that drives the successful entrepreneur towards greater and greater personal achievement. Many companies, both large and small, behave equally competitively in their corporate style. However, this rarely extends to the personal lives of the people involved. Corporate attitudes can change with time and aggressive companies may become complacent as they achieve success. Entrepreneurs, by comparison, never seem to loose their appetite for new competitive challenges—nor their willingness to compete at the personal as well as the corporate level.

The balance of the argument appears to favor the view that entrepreneurs have an abnormally developed need for their achievements to both within their control and recognized by the world at large. This "desire for applause" often results in a deep sense of dissatisfaction when the goal itself is obtained. The reason is simple: the value placed on winning by the entrepreneur is very often not accepted by either the people with whom he competes or the team who work with him. They fail to share with him the obsessional desire to succeed and hence the euphoria of winning. Consequently, success itself has a different value and the successful entrepreneur can find that he has a hollow victory on his hands. He usually finds this extremely irritating.

The sporting analogy is helpful once again. If you have competed with someone who is taking the game more seriously than the friendly context requires, you are likely to admire his success but dislike the individual for his attitude toward the competition. This can be equally true in business. It is a difficult challenge for the entrepreneur to be both a winner and achieve the genuine applause he will expect from those around him. It can be done, however, if the winner is mature and self-confident enough to see success in the context of a wider business perspective. It is sometimes a mark of an entrepreneur's coming of age that he tempers his natural inclination to trumpet his achievements at every possible opportunity.

## Failure? Who cares!

There is an interesting, almost fundamental, difference in attitude towards business failure in Europe and in the United States. In European countries, business failure is regarded as a major setback in an individual's career. It is seen as not just an unfortunate consequence of the risk-taking process but as prima facie evidence of a fundamental weakness in the person's character. By comparison, the attitude toward failure in the United States is quite different. Entrepreneurs are expected (if not required) to have suffered setbacks and failures as a part of the process of their development as individuals. Business failure is regarded as an essential part of the educational process of an individual ultimately destined to be successful. Risk-taking, whether at personal or corporate level, is seen to be a desirable and necessary part of wealth creation. The higher the risk, the greater the return expected. While this is equally true of his European counterpart, the American entrepreneur appears to have more understanding support from his backers, through both good times and bad. Higher rewards are expected from success (bankers are much larger and more willing company shareholders), but failures are not a cause of major anguish—they are simply seen as a necessary feature of the system.

The apparently more conservative approach to failure in Europe suggests greater problems for the entrepreneur in getting his new enterprise off the ground. Although this is now less the case than it was some years ago, it is undoubtedly true that a smaller proportion of ultimately successful European businessmen emerge from backgrounds of individual failure than is the case in the United States.

This issue is much influenced by the differing cultures and institutions of the two continents. Many American entrepreneurs emerge from a "blue-collar" background. By contrast, a study of the British entrepreneur conducted in 1988 (by Cranfield School of Management and Arthur Young) indicated that most of the entrepreneurs in their sample came from families in which the father had some type of small firm or self-employed experience. The educational and social influences, therefore, have a bearing on the differing attitudes toward failure.

Despite these differences, research suggests that entrepreneurs worldwide share an ability to shake off failure and to start again with a new venture. In the process, many entrepreneurs have the capability to attribute the failure to others rather than themselves. This "buck passing" seems to be part of a process of insulating the individual from the inevitable self-criticism which would otherwise follow the collapse of the enterprise. Typically, the entrepreneur will blame third parties such as suppliers, bankers, professional managers, or accountants who form part of his team. The accusations of misjudgment, incompetence, or downright disloyalty are usually expressed in vivid and unequivocal terms. In this way, the entrepreneur preserves his self-esteem (without any particular friends in the process) along with his ability to fight another day.

It is probably an oversimplification to suggest that entrepreneurs do not fear failure with as much passion as they wish for success. The fear itself can be a powerful motivator, but there is seldom evidence of it other than through a further adrenaline charge to their generally optimistic approach to the world. Those close to successful entrepreneurs know how much they agonize in private over things that have gone wrong. This is rarely seen in public and never by those on whom the entrepreneur depends for support or patronage.

Although the entrepreneur's attitude toward failure may at first appear to be cavalier, it can also be regarded as a subconscious reaction to an essential learning process. A child learns about the world by experimenting with it. If one attempt to do something produces failure or pain, another approach is tried, and so on until an effective solution is found. The entrepreneur's impatience to achieve things quickly makes him perhaps more "accident prone" than his more cautious colleagues.

Although the effect may be educational, the intention of the entrepreneur is unquestionably quite otherwise. It is also arguable whether or not he accepts and recognizes what others would conventionally call failure as just that. The very nature of the unconventional way in which entrepreneurs behave makes the commonplace epithets of success and failure generally less applicable to them. In this sense, the entrepreneur sets himself apart from his more conservative colleagues, purely because in some mysterious way he seems able to bend, if not break, the rules of conventional life.

## Breaking the rules

To be competitive, the entrepreneur frequently feels that he has to manipulate the environment around him to improve the odds oᶠ his success. He wants to mark the cards to give him a more favorable chance of winning the game. Indeed, there is a fine line between what is legal (but normally reprehensible) and what is downright dishonest. The old saying that "every great fortune is founded on a lie" contains more than a grain of truth when applied to the fruits of the work of entrepreneurs.

The instinct to shorten the odds by breaking the rules is often no more than a manifestation of a deep suspicion of, or an antipathy toward, anything institutional. It is this very refusal to be bound by the rules that often gives the entrepreneur his competitive edge. What appears to be the genius of highly successful individuals is in fact sometimes no more than a willingness to think from first principles about the nature of a particular problem in order to find a highly unconventional solution.

A famous historical example is the genius that led the Rothschilds to steal a march over their banking contemporaries at the time of the battle of Waterloo. Conventionally, news of victory or defeat in battle was carried by a courier from the battlefield—a process often taking several days, given the state of the roads and sea travel at that time. The Rothschilds realized that there was an alternative means of communication, namely the carrier pigeon. By this means the news of the victory was conveyed in secret to London a day before the conventional reports were received. Stock bought cheaply on rumors of a defeat was sold at massive profits days later when the victory was generally known. Ingenuity, or simply a willingness to reconsider the ground rules? Whatever the cause, the effect transformed communications thereafter.

A willingness to break the rules in information-gathering is a common feature of entrepreneurial behavior. How do entrepreneurs learn about competitive behavior, for example? They, or their staff, get to know the competitors' employees: they frequent the same pubs, sporting clubs, or societies; they approach executives through headhunters and in the process of offering a job to the prospective candidate learn about their competitors' business. They obtain information about their competitors' activities from their own customers and ask them to pass on any information, such as house journals, price lists, and product information which they may receive. Stopping short of industrial espionage, the entrepreneur is prepared to use unconventional and unexpected ways of gathering data to obtain a competitive advantage.

The founder of one consulting firm, McKinsey Strategic Management came up with a novel way to win a major new client when, in its early stages of development, it was crucial for the business to win a significant account. He rented an apartment next door to that of the owner of his target client and made sure that they met morning and evening as his neighbor left for, and returned from, his office.

This informal contact quickly led to a meeting over dinner at which McKinsey was able to make his business proposal. His competitors, bidding for business through the conventional methods, were outmaneuvered. This ingenious piece of advantage gaining also quickly changed the methods of selling in that sector of the market.

When launching new products or services, the entrepreneur will exploit every opportunity to sell benefits that differentiate the venture from competitors—but not always successfully. In the 1970s, Freddy Laker pioneered the concept of cheap international air travel, offering the prospect of foreign vacations to an enormous new and untapped market. His entry into that activity promised to create competitive disruption and it appeared for some time that the new enterprise would take the aviation business by storm. Despite the ultimate failure of the venture, the role of Freddy Laker as "people's champion" is now part of the mythology of the aviation industry. Later operators such as Richard Branson have in many senses been the inheritors of this earlier innovative and rule-breaking initiative.

## Concert parties

Even if a new idea has the most startling and obvious commercial potential to the entrepreneur, he often has to persuade others with more conservative views that the project is viable. The technique commonly used is that of creating an unstoppable momentum for a project by forming what is often called a concert party. In its crudest form, this is simply a manipulation of people's natural desire not to be left out when there is a good thing going. In its more sophisticated manifestation, the entrepreneur understands and manipulates these motives in a very subtle way. A hypothetical situation will illustrate how this is done.

A promoter, Joe Smith, sees the opportunity for an on-line translation service for medium-sized companies. He realizes that such companies increasingly do business in foreign countries but have few in-house language skills. Tender documents, correspondence, and product literature is commonly referred to local teachers or trade associations for translation, involving time delays and sometimes inadequate understanding of the technical terms used. He envisages a central bureau staffed by experienced linguists using advanced computer techniques to record and recall dictionaries of terms in many languages. The bureau would be linked to individual companies through fax or computer networks, so that the customer would be charged both an annual subscription and transaction fee, depending on the extent to which they used the bureau.

The concept is simple and potentially highly profitable. However, it needs a considerable amount of capital, the support of a "core" of company users and the availability of sufficient numbers of translators of the required quality. There are, therefore, three quite distinct groups of people whom the entrepreneur must persuade before the project can start, namely financiers, customers, and translators.

Joe starts by talking to companies. He paints a glowing picture of the scale and efficiency of the service, mentions the names of several of their competitors who are interested and promises both cost saving and competitive advantage. He also seeks permission to use their names as potentially interested customers. The companies concerned see little to lose in showing support in principle since they have no contractual obligation. In addition, they are also anxious not to lose out to competitors when promised some degree of exclusivity. Their names are, of course, used by Joe when visiting his next potential customer in such a way that they should like very enthusiastic supporters of the venture.

Joe then tracks down his potential translators. He tells them that he has the venture almost set up and that he can promise them an interesting and rewarding career. He fills them with enthusiasm at the prospect of senior management appointments and early promotion and gives them a foretaste of share option schemes and capital profit. Carried away by Joe's infectious enthusiasm, they cannot wait to sign up.

Armed with these credentials, Joe talks to his potential financiers. He plays the field by involving more than one investor. He hints to each that one of the others is more advanced in the negotiations and can offer better terms. He quotes the venture as a *fait accompli* and his staff as though they were already hired. He has found the premises, the lease must be signed in three days, a major customer has an urgent contract to fulfill . . . Many other similar devices are used to hustle the deal. Joe only needs to put one of the pieces in place to increase the likelihood of assembling the others. He creates an atmosphere of excitement and momentum and, with any luck, the concert party is soon gathered.

As Joe will find, the most difficult person he has to persuade to join in this communal wish fulfillment is the financier, streetwise and case-hardened, who approaches every deal with studied care and caution. Even these prudent individuals, however, have been known to get carried away on the entrepreneurial bandwagon. The high failure rate of new ventures, which is widely accepted by the financing community, must in part be accounted for by this factor.

◆　◆　◆

## The wild ones

By breaking establishment rules, sailing close to the wind and being generally unpredictable, many entrepreneurs get a reputation for being less than respectable. Any market that has become institutionalized and comfortable is fair game for the raiding entrepreneur. In such a situation, competitors commonly observe a strong unwritten ethical code. This is not to suggest that cartels exist, but rather that a state of gentlemanly equilibrium is observed between competing parties. Whoever is bold enough to challenge this ordered situation will inevitably be branded as, at best, a disreputable maverick. This description is almost always unfair and no more than a cry of pain from those whose cozy world is challenged, perhaps for the first time.

It was an entrepreneurial initiative that shook the established world of the main street grocery stores with the coming of the supermarket; ship owners were caught on the wrong foot by the introduction of the container ship and the supertanker; and the ingenuity and aggression of Japanese electronics manufacturers shocked many European companies into a sudden awareness of their own innate weakness.

Acting as a catalyst for radical change in such mature and well-established situations, the entrepreneur is bound to find himself regarded as ungentlemanly and his activities unwelcome. The interesting question is whether entrepreneurs intentionally seek such confrontation with the established order, or whether it is an incidental feature of their drive to succeed.

Research into the attitudes of entrepreneurs in the United States and Europe suggests that they feel deeply uneasy in a well-ordered setting. Many entrepreneurs drop out of school early or find themselves at odds with the boss in a working context. They have the reputation of being "against the system," questioning decisions, and making life difficult for their superiors. They demonstrate their independence through many, apparently trivial, aspects of their behavior: at school, they may be poor attenders, insolent to teachers or leaders of playground gangs; at work, they may have the tiresome habits of questioning decisions, poking their noses into aspects of the business which do not immediately concern them, and making trouble on the shop floor; in their leisure time, they may seek activities that involve potential conflict with authority. While this non-conformist approach to life varied in degree of prominence between entrepreneurs, as a general rule it appears to be one of their distinguishing characteristics. Certainly, those who have been successful in the long term often show this predilection to challenge the established order to a high degree.

## A feeling of unimportance?

Some psychologists have argued that entrepreneurs need to reassure themselves constantly of their importance in the world. In a sense, this is a manifestation of a deeply-felt inferiority complex. By taking on challenging and risky situations, the entrepreneur draws attention to himself and thereby enhances his self-esteem. Although this analysis has some merit (and experience suggests that entrepreneurs are not always the bold, confident individuals that they project themselves to be) there seems an equal likelihood that the motive is as much mischievous as attention-seeking. The pure pleasure an entrepreneur can gain from the discomfiture of those whom he regards as established and self-satisfied has to be seen to be believed. It is this iconoclasm which often makes entrepreneurs exciting and agreeable to work with.

The "magnificent obsession" that spurs entrepreneurs on to break the rules can also lead them into darker areas of deceit and wrongdoing. There is a line entrepreneurs sometimes find very difficult to discern between "conduct unbecoming to a gentleman" and conduct that can lead to a prison cell. It is very easy, when challenging the established order, to create a personal set of rules that stray over this narrow line. Trading practices that may be unconventional but acceptable are quite different from those that break the law. This is not to suggest that entrepreneurs are less ethical or honest than anyone else. It is simply that they place themselves in situations where the temptation to act dishonestly is greater than usual.

For example, an entrepreneurial property developer seeking planning consent for a speculative investment in land that has stretched his financial resources may well be tempted to go beyond simple persuasion when dealing with council officials. His entrepreneurial drive has put him into the situation where the issue of one person's attitude to the transaction may be crucial to his future. This self-imposed pressure does, sometimes, lead the entrepreneur toward the slippery slope of illegal behavior. Part of his difficulty may be the lack either of an external set of values to which he adheres sufficiently strongly or the confidence in an advisor who has such values. This in itself can be a product of the entrepreneur's tendency to be a nonconformist. Thus, he may find himself in a position where his judgment of what is right or wrong in a situation is conditioned more by his own view of the world than by an dispassionate analysis of legality. The "crimes" committed by entrepreneurs are probably more associated with misrepresentation through exaggeration than culpable acts of dishonesty. In this respect, they have only themselves to blame for their often poor public image.

In most things, the entrepreneur is a risk-taker. Finding a competitive edge or a novel approach to a problem involved assessing risks. How does the entrepreneur go about this vital process?

## Knowing the odds

Every businessman knows that the assessment of a commercial risk is an art rather than a science. Although economists, mathematicians, and accountants can offer powerful techniques to illuminate the decision, the final judgment is inevitably subjective. The reason is simple: the world is highly complex and political, economic, and commercial forces interplay both nationally and internationally in ways that remain poorly understood. Any enterprising venture, whether by an individual or a corporation, inevitably involves uncertainty associated with forces well beyond rational analysis. All businessmen must use whatever intellectual skills they have in understanding analytical data to complement their powers of subjective judgment. In sporting terms, the businessman is thereby taking the best view he can of the odds of success against failure. The entrepreneur must address the same issues to reach his own conclusions on the potential for success. His approach, however, often differs radically from that used in large corporations. It generally has the following features:

- Extremely sensitive understanding of customer behavior.
- A strongly visualized understanding of operating parameters.
- A very detailed (and often cautious) assessment of downside risks.

Each of these is worth examining in more detail.

## Knowing the customer

The entrepreneur's customers may be companies or individuals and the product or the service offered may be an exploitation of an existing idea or the introduction of a new one. There may be a few, highly specialized, potential buyers or every teenager with money in his pocket—the permutations are endless. The successful entrepreneur has gained an insight into the way the market is likely to behave *after* his project is launched, not just how it behaves today.

There are three distinctive ways in which this sensitivity to the customer's need is achieved:

1. Keen observation of human behavior.
2. An eclectic interest in information.
3. A powerful imagination.

The ability to be a keen observer does not necessarily involve high intellect; it is more an inborn sense of curiosity. Spotting a business opportunity, as discussed earlier, requires an acute sense of the "missing links" or inconsistencies in the way things are presently done. This same sensitive power of observation also feeds the judgmental processes involved in risk-taking. The entrepreneur is almost like a medieval explorer stepping for the first time onto the shores of an unknown continent: he has a heightened awareness of his surroundings because they are both alien and potentially both exciting and dangerous. The entrepreneur, always questioning the existing order, could be seen to have heightened perception for a not dissimilar reason. By contrast, those whose inclination is more toward a comfortable conformity are less likely to be acute observers of human behavior. They expect people to behave in predictable ways and rarely question the degree to which changed opportunities will themselves result in different behavior patterns.

Of course, it is the behavioral observations that are crucial. Many entrepreneurial plans are based on what appears to be the wholly rational—"If I can make this product with more features than my competitors for 10 percent less, I will sell a hundred thousand a year." In the long run such rational arguments are often totally valid, so that the replacement of the old-style bicycle by the current two-wheeler was an inevitable consequence of the superior efficiency of the latter. The flaw lies in the assumption of rationality in the short term, over which period entrepreneurial success or failure is frequently measured.

Even in the most apparently clinical and quantified areas of business, such as banking, insurance and stock brokerage, buying behavior, when it comes to innovation, is determined by factors other than the purely rational. An individual's judgment on whether to follow an innovative lead will be determined by many things—not least by his innate conservatism or radicalism, the choices of competitors and peer group members, the internal politics of the vested interest in his own organization, and so on. At the individual level, the dictates of fashion and snob appeal are often more powerful influences over consumer choices than anything that would otherwise be a rational determinant. Thus, anyone associated with innovation must reckon with these irrational elements in human behavior. By keenly observing the way people behave in one set of circumstances, the entrepreneur can better predict how they will behave in another. An example will serve to illustrate this point.

◆    ◆    ◆

Ted Tweedle has invented the ultimate robot, the electronic manservant, which will not only do the housework to your oral commands but will serve drinks to your guests, tell bedtime stories to the children, and dig the garden. The price is steep, but the potential market is huge. Ted's problem: how to make some accurate prediction of how quickly his product will take off. A crucial issue is how the robot is sold; it can be retailed through chain stores, sold in the customer's own home, or marketed by mail order. Each selling situation suggests a different behavioral response, so Ted uses his observation of analogous situations to decide which would be best.

He has observed that the larger domestic items are bought from retail stores by husband and wife together. The wife, as primary user, normally leads the choice with the husband as the final arbiter and paymaster. In the home setting, by contrast, the husband is usually the dominant individual in the buying process, perhaps because there is a subconscious assumption that he will act more dominantly in his own domain. Lastly, he knows that selling large items by mail order lacks any "feel" beyond what the customer (husband or wife) sees on the printed page.

His experience tells him that the buying decision is more likely to be made by the husband than the wife. Quite apart from the cost of the robot, he observe that, if a radical change is involved, the person with most potential to benefit is often the most reluctant to initiate the change. He, therefore, seeks the setting in which he can maximize the likelihood of the husband making a positive buying decision. He bases his assumptions, therefore, on the sale of the robot to potential customers in their own homes.

◆    ◆    ◆

40

## The information gatherer

The ability to observe behavior keenly and in detail is often complemented by a broad-ranging affection for collecting data. Recent research has shown that successful business leaders ask between 500 and 1,000 questions during an average working day. These questions are asked not only of immediate subordinates, but also of a huge network of people both inside and outside the organization. The quality of absorbing what may seem to be irrelevant data from all sorts of sources, storing it away, and being able to retrieve it when needed is a very recognizable trait. Many entrepreneurs read very little; most seem to read less and less the more successful they become. They rely on what they hear or see with their own eyes. Some commit little to writing and appear to distrust anything that cannot be expressed in strong and simple language.

These two qualities of keen observation and eclectic interest in information-gathering is often coupled with a powerful imagination. Entrepreneurs do not need to be imaginative in the wholly creative sense of that word. Much of entrepreneurialism is concerned with exploiting opportunities and ideas derived from those of others. However, the power of imagination applies to a more logical process, which flows directly from these two other talents. Thus, for example, the promoter of a new chain of ethnic restaurants might visualize not only the sort of customers to whom the food would appeal, but also the physical location, the interior door, the style of service, the promotional campaign and so on. Very often, it is that imaginative power which gives the entrepreneur the ability to exploit ideas that have lain dormant after the initial phase of invention. It is almost as though the creative process becomes spent and a new innovative charge is needed. The imagination of the entrepreneur must not stop short at the product itself—it has to visualize the ultimate use and its associated revenue flow.

## Seeing all the parts

There is risk attached to every aspect of a new venture. The old adage has it that "the battle was lost for the want of a horseshoe nail." Similarly, a business venture can be wrecked by the failure of an apparently insignificant but vital element. Any complex new product is likely to involve a variety of technologies and sources of supply. Poor quality, late delivery, or unexpectedly high costs of any can be disastrous. Unsuccessful ventures in recent years in three-dimensional photography and "fourth generation" television are striking examples.

The successful entrepreneur must not only understand the individual elements of his project, but he must also have the ability to see them as the interlinked parts of a complete enterprise. A vital element is the collaborators, managers and employees who will bring the idea to fruition. The entrepreneur must perceive both their individual roles and also the way in which they are likely to relate to each other. He must face the risks of poor recruitment as much as the possibility of a supplier or subcontractor letting him down.

The process involved in refining this operating model goes on largely inside the entrepreneur's head. It appears to be a series of postulations based on adjusting one factor at a time considering the consequences of that on the project as a whole. For example, he may consider the effects of making a product in-house or simply assembling bought-in components. What effect will this have on factory management, stock levels, customer deliveries, finance requirements, profit margins, and so on? Next, he will consider part manufactured and part bought-in components and go through the same sequence of considerations. Some variations will have several dimensions of influence on the venture. Choosing to sell direct or through wholesalers is one illustration of how a venture will differ fundamentally in its operation. It is a complex process which has been likened to solving the problems of four-dimensional chess. What may appear to an outsider to be a near-miraculous feat of organization when a project is started is often merely a manifestation of this highly detailed and time-consuming thought process which has been going on in the entrepreneur's mind for some time. We will look in a later chapter at the role of the entrepreneur as a planner and manager; in many ways this ability to "exploit" a concept, which the original inventor perhaps found too difficult, is one of his key differentiating skills.

It is rare to find this process either fully documented or employing conventional risk measurement methods. Once again, the entrepreneur's judgment of how people in a new context are likely to react is an essential element. As most management scientists would agree, the uncertainty involved is considerable. The entrepreneur relies on the information gathering and assessment of needs we discussed earlier as a vital ingredient in this process. It must also be both comprehensive and thorough down to the finest detail. For example, launching a new product might involve the following key elements:

- Securing the supply in adequate quantities and to reliable quality of all key components.
- Finding a suitable manufacturing location and facilities.

- Recruiting suitably expert management and training a labor force.

- Obtaining the necessary funds both to start the venture and to finance it through its initial launch period.

- Devising marketing and selling plans and preparing launch campaigns.

- Conducting relevant market research to confirm the entrepreneur's assessment of the likely uptake of a new product.

- Maintaining the maximum secrecy practicable before the launch itself.

Although the auto industry is dominated by large manufacturers, the preparation and launch of a new model involves many of these elements. Using this analogy, it is clear that failure to anticipate and deal with difficulties in any of these areas could be both costly and potentially crucial to the success of the enterprise.

Every project is, of course, different in its complexity, and there are many illustrations of entrepreneurial ventures that are no more than "acorns," where the principle of a modest test launch is the most viable approach. Even there, however, the entrepreneur who has not thought through all the aspects of the venture is running additional risks, not only on his own behalf but also for those who are backing him. It is the person with the capacity to see all the parts of a venture and to review how each interacts with the other who is most likely to succeed. The techniques used are sometimes referred to as "scenario planning," and many corporate strategies are now based on the more formal use of this technique. It is an interesting illustration of how the entrepreneurial model infects the management disciplines used by those involved in more mature businesses.

### Assessing the downside

Entrepreneurs are commonly assumed to be risk-takers to the extent that they are willing to gamble on any situation. It is sometimes cynically suggested that they are more than happy to play with other people's money, with the object of achieving both self-esteem and exceptional gain. Gambling can involve either a blind faith in good fortune or a close assessment of risks. Experience suggests that most entrepreneurs are remarkably cautious in their approach to risk-taking, despite the fact that the initiatives they take are seen by others as bold and adventurous.

The reason for this paradox is that the conscious or subconscious analysis the entrepreneur makes when he is looking forward to a new project involves a process of confidence-building based on his own judgment. There is a regular reassessment of the downside risk involved in the project; the exposure involved should any part of the project fail is quantified and, if appropriate, accumulated with those relating to other elements.

In the case illustrated on the following page, the risk analysis is being undertaken for a contractor who is aware that there are various major factors affecting finishing the job on time (each of these is listed at the foot of the chart). The vertical axis measures the probability of an even occurring by a particular date—when it is 0 the event cannot occur before then and when it reaches 1 it is certain to occur.

Each of the six factors is considered in turn, the measurement of the probability of each being *added* to produce a combined maximum delay for the project as a whole until the end of September. The intersection between the base plan completion data line and line 6 (representing the accumulated risk) intersects at 0.2 indicating that there is only a 20 percent chance that the contractor will be able to complete his project on time. He must then decide whether to accept the degree of risk involved, negotiate a new, later completion date or renegotiate the penalties for late completion of the contract.

The diagram on page 46 in graphical form how the risk inherent in a project can be measured and the cumulative effect judged.

Risk-management techniques are commonly used in civil engineering projects, for example in the building of a dam. Before the project starts there are uncertainties about the soil conditions to be encountered, the weather during the construction period, the volume of materials needed to construct the dam to a given height, the possibility of labor unrest, and so on. The risk-measurement technique involves a very scientific and careful assessment of previous experience in other projects, the judgment of experts and the expression of the results in terms of statistical confidence levels. By aggregating the risk assessments, an overall risk coefficient can be calculated for the project and converted into a bracket of both time and project cost. If the project is destined to be directly revenue-earning, such as a new toll bridge, the risk-assessment model can be linked directly to the income assumptions. Thus, a delay in the completion date of a project both extends the expenditure period and reduces the net present value of the income because it is received later than originally planned. These differences alter, in turn, the expected rate of return on the project and may indeed reach a point at which its viability comes into question.

Whatever method is used, the promoter of a project must see a *comparative* risk-reward ratio that is acceptable to him. In the case of a project being considered by a mature company, there are two criteria by which this measurement is made:

1. The external opportunities to invest at a comparable level of risk.
2. Competing internal projects.

If a company is considering whether or not to invest in the development and launch of a new product with an 80 percent chance of success, then it must show at least a 20 percent better return on capital than, say, a totally safe investment in government bonds. Equally, if there is competition in the company between two possible ventures, the one offering the more attractive risk-reward equation will normally be chosen. In this way, commercial judgments in established companies are, in theory at least, justified in terms of both offering a better return than an alternative external investment and the best internal candidate available. In practice, there are often much broader and more subjective issues of corporate strategy involved in investment decisions than this rather mechanical approach would suggest. It nonetheless remains an essentially comparative process and it is this which provides the insight into the way in which the entrepreneur approaches risk.

Richard Branson, when describing his own approach to risk, says that he keeps each of his enterprises small and never takes a business risk that would put any of his other ventures in jeopardy. This limiting of the downside is, in his case, the feature of a well-organized and mature entrepreneurial business. When a new business is started the downside is often the financial ruin of the entrepreneur—indeed, those supporting a new venture expect the promoter to back it with all his available capital, time, and energy. It would seem logical that an entrepreneur, faced with the apparently huge risk, would only choose those ventures which offered an exceptional payback. Optimistic self-delusion, however, can infect the judgment of the entrepreneur to the extent that he dismisses risk and sees nothing but immeasurable reward. Perhaps in some cases irrational self-confidence turns the venture that flies in the face of common sense into a historic success story. However, for every case in which this happens there are a thousand where it doesn't.

The first venture which an entrepreneur undertakes is almost certainly motivated more by the very strong ambition of the individual to become independent and recognized by those around him as a success

## Cumulative risk profile

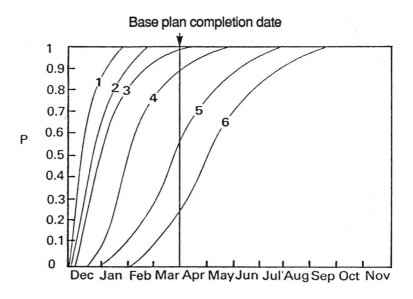

FIFTH YEAR

Cumulative probability distribution with six risk source components for a construction project. The components are:

1. Yard not available/mobilization problems
2. Construction problems/adverse weather
3. Late delivery of subcontracted items
4. Material delivery delays
5. Industrial disputes
6. Delayed award of contract

P = probability coefficient where 1 = certainty

Adapted from Cooper & Chapman, *Risk Analysis for Large Projects*, 1986.
Reprinted by permission of John Wiley & Sons, Ltd.

than by any more rational considerations. Measured by external alternatives, these first entrepreneurial ventures appear to be poor investments. Indeed, many fail, and the venture capitalist is fortunate if, out of his portfolio of ten start-ups, two achieve really significant growth over five years. The 20 percent who are successful may have a better proposition, be more capable businessmen, or simply have more good fortune than the others; or it may be that they are just more skillful in assessing the risks and organizing their projects accordingly. The entrepreneurs who survive this first venturing phase and prosper rarely need to take comparable levels of risk as the venture matures. Their success attracts opportunities for *leverage*, which becomes the key to making an acceptable return on investment a truly exceptional one.

"Leverage" is the term used to describe the relationship between the equity capital invested in a venture and borrowed money. The equity capital is wholly at risk and is entirely lost if the venture fails. Borrowed money, on the other hand, frequently has some underpinning security to which the lender can have recourse if the venture gets into trouble. In the earlier stages of the entrepreneur's career, he is unproven and his ideas, however, excellent, will be treated as being more risky than when he has proved his success. As a consequence, his opportunities for borrowing are significantly limited in relation to his own capital.

As he demonstrates his business capability he will attract a following from those who are willing to lend on a substantial basis in return for, perhaps, a small part of the equity. Suppose, for example, that the entrepreneur needs to raise ten million dollars for his new venture; five million might be covered by some security (say land and buildings), the remaining five million being largely at risk. If he is established and successful he might do a deal on the basis of, say, a million dollars of his own money plus four million of loan capital, which could, at the option of the lender, be converted into 10 percent of the equity of the company. This option will be worth exercising if the value of the company exceeds forty million dollars, since the 10 percent equity stake will be worth more than the value of the repayment of the loan. At that stage, the entrepreneur's original one-million-dollar stake would be worth thirty-six million dollars, since he still owns 90 percent of the equity. Up to the point when the option to convert is exercised, the entrepreneur enjoys *all* the equity value even though he has only put up effectively one-fifth of the risk capital.

The more successful the entrepreneur, the greater the opportunity he has to use the leverage effect and the smaller the proportion of equity incentive that he needs to offer his backers. In theory, he can take greater and greater risks since his own proportion of the investment is so small. In practice, however, the house of cards can easily collapse if the entrepreneur does not sustain his reputation as "a winner." This brings us back to Richard Branson's approach of restricting downside risks to manageable units. It underlines the reality of the caution successful entrepreneurs bring in practice to their investment decisions. They are, in effect, hugely aware of the penalty in terms of borrowing capacity that follows in the wake of failure. If their investments are highly leveraged, they do not have to seek the level of risk-reward ratio needed by those who lack that reputation. This, perhaps, explains the paradox of the cautious entrepreneur.

## Summary

The entrepreneur has an instinctive and powerful urge to compete. He will seek any feasible way to obtain competitive advantage and is a natural rule-breaker. He is prepared to "sail close to the wind" and use unconventional persuasive techniques. In the last analysis, however, the idea of the entrepreneur as a person who always takes high risks is a myth. The leverage which the entrepreneur can bring to the use of his own capital is the key to his sustaining success while being both thorough and cautious in his assessment of viable projects.

*Chapter 4*

# Individualist

Entrepreneurs thrive on being visible. They like to be "up front," setting the pace and being recognized. When successful, they welcome the public awareness that follows. Do such men set out to be different, and if so, what is the mainspring of this drive? Is it, perhaps, that the process of unrelenting competition sharpens and accentuates their individuality? Or are they simply playing out some heroic myth—a source of personal destiny determining the course of the individual's life and career?

The answers to these questions lie deep in the distinctive psychology of the entrepreneur. Although differing in degree of emphasis, the results of academic research and those of ordinary observation confirm that there are many common features. In this chapter these are reviewed and explored.

## The rebellious urge
Entrepreneurs generally rebel against rules and authority, whether in school or in the workplace. As Kets de Vries* comments:

"While managers seem able to identify in a positive and constructive way with authority figures using them as role models, many of the entrepreneurs I have observed lack the managers' fluidity in changing from a superior to a subordinate role; instead they often experience structure as stifling. They find it very difficult to work with others in structured situations unless, of course, *they* created the structure and the work is done on *their* terms."

---

* "The Dark Side of Entrepreneurship" (*Harvard Business Review* November-December 1985).

This lack of tolerance of, and impatience with, the conventional is a recurrent and market feature of entrepreneurs. This does not suggest that all rebels are entrepreneurs, but a degree of willingness to "buck the system" and challenge authority is a recognizable part of the entrepreneur's make-up. Stories abound of nascent entrepreneurs who were the terrors of their classrooms, universities, or workplaces. Disobedience, disloyalty, and a tendency to be at the forefront in any disruptive behavior are all regularly reported attributes of such youthful mavericks.

There are two schools of thought about why such behavior occurs. One suggests that the individual has an inborn rebellious urge and the other that it results from "conditioning." The first draws on evidence indicating that a high proportion of entrepreneurs display this tendency at such an early age that the conventional social factors (class, family background, economic circumstances, and so on) have had little, if any, opportunity to be a real influence. They also point out that entrepreneurs spring from a wide variety of backgrounds and few common influences seem to be at work. The "conditioners" use evidence that entrepreneurs are more often "incubated" in some environments than others. For example, companies that are themselves entrepreneurial are more likely to spawn individuals with that characteristic than those with a more bureaucratic outlook. Both schools agree that entrepreneurs are confident, self-reliant individuals who have a higher "locus of control" than people generally. They "believe that success depends on their own efforts, instead of seeing themselves as victims of luck, chance or fate."[*]

Those who support the conditioning theory argue that the circumstances that create the entrepreneurial opportunity must not only be propitious for some new initiative, but also exactly right as far as the individual is concerned. In effect, the entrepreneur has to be in the right place at the right time in his career for the magic to work. Without this "accidental" coincidence of opportunity, man and the moment, the prospective entrepreneur never emerges as a real one.

It seems that neither school has a complete and convincing answer. The population of entrepreneurs is as wide as the nature and scale of the enterprises in which they are involved. Within the terms of the definition used in this book, however, successful entrepreneurs seem not only to have an abnormal inclination to be rebellious, but also to have shown this trait from an early age. This suggests that there is,

[*] Longenecker, McKinney & Moore, "Egoism & Independence: Entrepreneurial Ethics" (*Organization Dynamics*, October 1988). Reprinted by permission of publisher ©1988. American Management Association, New York. All rights reserved.

50

perhaps, more of an inherited process at work than an externally created one.

Whether entrepreneurs are born or made, the fact is that they are often difficult employees and unpredictable workmates. Again, there are three basic explanations, which can be broadly described as:

- The applause theory.
- The insecurity theory.
- The "other world" syndrome.

### Applause-seeking

This theory suggests that the rebellious entrepreneur is motivated by the adulation that challenging the conventional order will win him among his peers. He has a deep fear of being "ordinary," of not standing out from the crowd, and consequently seeks every opportunity to put himself forward. The action may be reckless, spontaneous and even against his own interest but it is, nevertheless, instinctive. Thus, for example, the entrepreneur may set out to shock or outrage his audience if that is the only way of being visible. At a dinner party, the self-made man will want to be heard. If the conversation is out of his field or his fellow guests are standoffish, he will as soon say or do something offensive (insulting the host or committing some other *faux pas*) as not do anything at all. The wife of such a person will testify to the agonies of uncertainty that can precede such events.

Being "applauded," therefore, does not only mean being congratulated or admired: the applause-seeker gains the same satisfaction from being able to say, "That showed them," as "They loved me!" Not all entrepreneurs are as boorish and publicity-seeking as this analysis would suggest, but there seem to be few successful entrepreneurs who are reluctant to stand out from the crowd. It can be argued, of course, that applause-seeking is no more than another manifestation of the entrepreneur's deeply competitive instinct. It seems that what is instinctive becomes habitual, in terms of social and business behavior, and it is this feature that results in so many entrepreneurs being disagreeable companions.

### The insecurity factor

The second explanation for this rebelliousness is that the entrepreneur is so deeply insecure in his relationship with the world that his actions are aimed at giving him regular reassurance of his importance in it. It is rather like someone walking through a darkened room: hands and feet seek contact, any contact, with the furniture, walls, and doors to give a sense of reality to the experience. The insecure individual can, of course, react to this feeling by withdrawing into an increasingly personal inner world, but such introversion is very rare in entrepreneurs. The action that gives rise to the desired reassurance is less relevant than the fact that it takes place. Being noticed is more easily achieved through doing something extreme than through doing something essentially ordinary: the eccentric, iconoclastic, or rebellious act therefore comes more naturally than the conventional.

It would be foolish to suggest that entrepreneurs are somehow always abnormal or deviant in their psychological make-up, but it seem that many see the world or their personal position in it as somehow incongruous and hence needing correction. The insecurity theory is based on such a premise. The individual rebels less because he feels superior to others, but rather because of his discomfort at the *differences* he perceives, which others may not. Entrepreneurs seldom come across as insecure people although this characteristic sometimes emerges in later life when fortunes have been made and the competitive pace slackens. It may be that a natural gift for presentation and salesmanship disguises deeper worries than are publicly apparent.

## The "other world"

There is a theory that certain people see the world in very different terms from the rest of us. They have a comprehensive framework of beliefs, rules, expectations, and assumptions, which are internally consistent but tangential to those which most people accept and understand. The "Alice in Wonderland" logic of these other worlds is so self-evident to the individual that things which seem otherwise normal are, to them, extraordinary. Such "otherworldliness" can relate to ethics, value systems, personal relationships, loyalties, political attitudes, and numerous other aspects of life.

It is, of course, quite common to find individuals with strongly developed prejudices or personal beliefs. Thus, for example, someone may have a view of personal justice or ethical behavior which will verge on the extreme. He will stand up against authority when he perceives an injustice being done. He will subscribe to causes, agitate, offer himself for martyrdom, or do whatever is needed to pursue what he sees as being "right." Progress has often depended on the passion and commitment of such people, not least in the fields of religion, politics, and the law. Some entrepreneurs share such passions and, as discussed elsewhere, these are frequently the mainspring of their ability to innovate and wreak changes in the world around them.

A passionate set of beliefs about one set of issues does not, however, constitute the whole "other world." They are only a part of it. The other world as seen by the entrepreneur must be complete to satisfy this requirement. It would need coherent and consistent views on:

- The order of society and the role of the individual within it.
- What constitutes "good" and "bad" behavior.
- The destiny of the entrepreneur himself and the value of his powers and skills in relation to everyone else.
- A concept of the "correct" order of things against which actual experience can be measured.

It can be argued that despotic leaders have many of these delusions and live within a personal and very different set of values from the rest of us. The passionate commitment that they bring to their life's work is testament to the power of this vision. Entrepreneurs are, themselves, quite frequently described as despotic by their subordinates. In some cases, the description is used almost as a term of affection and, as much of history demonstrates, a substantial proportion of the human race accepts despotism willingly, if not enthusiastically.

What succeeds in politics or religion, however, is unlikely to succeed consistently in business. The "other world" theory ultimately fails the test of practicality. In the last analysis, the entrepreneur must deliver practical solutions through an understanding and exploitation of human behavior. Although the politician may also do this, his approach is fundamentally different. The entrepreneur must exploit the opportunities presented by a small part of an existing system. The politician seeks power through manipulating the rules of the system as a whole.

The answer to the question, "Why does the entrepreneur rebel?" lies not in any one of these theories but, to a greater or lesser extent, in all of them. His behavior may be irrational and challenging for many reasons, and as a result of complex inner and external pressures. The fact that such behavior is consistently found cannot be denied. Our ability to analyze its causes, however, remains imperfect.

## Who can you trust?
As fierce competitors, entrepreneurs, particularly early on in their careers, regard everyone as a potential rival. In the school playground, in the factory or office, or on the sports field, no quarter is sought or expected. A rival is naturally someone who is out to beat you and the last person with whom you share confidences. Experience of the world

quickly persuades the entrepreneur that games, whether sporting or commercial, are often not played according to the Queensberry rules. Respect for rivals becomes tinged with and then centered on distrust.

Two individuals may, for example, be bidding for the same piece of work or for the same business opportunity. They may or may not have competed before. Assume that they have broadly comparable solutions to offer at similar prices. The search for individual advantage is therefore likely to turn to other, less conventional considerations. In gaining such advantage, secrecy and surprise are often essential elements. Equally, diversionary tactics may be used. One bidder may leak to the other the fact that he is uninterested in the work or is bidding in the wrong way. Simultaneously, he may have a surprise element in the offing. (A major consulting assignment in Africa was won, for example, by one bidder promising to transport all the clients' senior executives and their wives to a week's training conference in Florida; their lower-priced competitors were totally unaware of this surprise tactic until it was too late.)

In situations such as this, the entrepreneur will distrust not only his competitors, but also many of his associates and advisors. Playing it close to the chest or "needing to know" is a common sense protection against sensitive information falling into the wrong hands. There are many cases, however, where the perceived need for secretary (and hence the implication of distrust) extends well beyond the boundaries of commercial necessity.

Beyond this narrow and well-defined area of commercial rivalry lies a wider spectrum of personal and commercial relationships in which the grounds for apparently distrusting those around the entrepreneur become more complex and fascinating. The extent of the distrust and hence the degree of loneliness seems to increase dramatically as the entrepreneur himself succeeds and accumulates wealth. The ultimate archetype is the reclusive multi-millionaire, trusting no one, believing himself to be the victim of a predatory conspiracy, miserable and unloved, finally dying unmourned by the rest of the world. Protecting one's hard-won wealth is usually regarded as a natural and creditable action. It is only in the extreme that it becomes somewhat pathetic.

Young, applause-seeking businessmen like to talk about the ventures and the successes they achieve. While they distrust rivals, they are avid information-gatherers and will often take complete strangers into their confidence if there is something to be gained. They seldom leave key tasks to others, although this probably has more to do with lack of confidence in their subordinates' competence than with doubts about their loyalty or motivation. In a sense they have little to lose and so take more conscious (and unconscious) risks.

As an empire grows and wealth is created, there is more to protect; the suspicion that people may be trying to cash in grows apace. The sense of distrust becomes deeply rooted and can extend as much to close relatives as to business associates. The motives of wives, children, uncles, aunts, nephews and nieces may be questioned in terms of their "getting their hands on my money!" What applies in the family is often seen in a more extreme way in business.

To counter his mistrust of others, the entrepreneur may divide information about his affairs among a number of people so that no one person can comprehend it all; he may run a management regime on the basis of frequent moves among senior personnel to ensure that no individual becomes too powerful for too long; he may constantly reorganize and restructure his businesses as much to confuse external inquirers as to make his affairs more efficient or tax-effective.

What often emerges in the single "confidant" who provides the exception to these general rules. There seems to be a curiously wide variety of individuals who play this role. In one real-life instance, it was a fortune-teller, visited monthly by the entrepreneur and privy to all his affairs. The lady concerned appeared to gain no personal advantage from the significant influence she exercised over her client despite the manifest opportunities available to her. In another (and probably more common) example, it was a long-standing personal secretary. Wives (or husbands) *should* automatically fall within this class but exceptions are extremely common. The trust implicit in the confidant relationship involves not only revelation of information, but also commentary on it. It may be that the entrepreneur's sense of consideration for his wife restricts him from worrying her with his business problems; or it may be that the very closeness of the personal relationship precludes objectivity in business matters.

In many cases, the confidant is someone who can be relied on but is seen to have no competitive or predatory motives. An old school friend, a retired businessman, a professional advisor, or a successful executive in a wholly unrelated activity may each meet these criteria. The loyalty which the entrepreneur displays to his confidant can be as absolute as and quite contrary to his apparent distrust of everyone else. Such relationships are often very long-lasting and have their roots early in the entrepreneur's career. While distrust of the world at large is generally an unappealing attribute, it has its compensations. A trusted friend and advisor, serving the entrepreneur over many years, sharing his successes and failures, can make up for a galaxy of unsatisfactory short-term relationships.

## Non-team playing

When carried to extremes, a sense of distrust of others can bring the entrepreneur problems in addition to loneliness and an unhappy personal life. It can, and does, bring enormous inefficiencies in the way businesses are organized and managed. The benefits that flow from powerful individualism can have opposite (and sometimes equal) penalties in terms of destroying teamwork.

When and why is teamwork important? Like many business concepts the element of teamwork needed in achieving a particular business goal varies dramatically according to the complexity of the situation. Take, for example, two extremes:

◆　◆　◆

Johnny (ten years old) discovers that he can buy candy in bulk at a local warehouse, split it into small bags and sell it at a 400 percent profit in the playground. His only "team" member is his mom, who provides the starter capital for the candy and the paper bags. Sole trader Johnny soon achieves financial independence and relies on no one other than himself. As his own boss, he can decide what to sell, how much to sell, how much to charge, and so on, entirely at his own discretion. The archetypal youthful millionaire in the making!

At the other extreme, NASA is determined to spend $20 billion putting a man on Mars. The project extends ten years, involves hundreds of main contractors, thousands of sub-contractors, and tens of thousands of component and service suppliers. While the scientific and engineering concepts of the project require innovation and experimentation, its execution demands order, precision, and reliability of quality and delivery. The scope for entrepreneurial flair and management eccentricity is limited to say the least, and effective teamwork between countries, companies and managers is of paramount importance.

◆　◆　◆

Recognizing that virtually all entrepreneurial activity lies between these extremes, the relationship between growth and the potential for entrepreneurial inefficiency caused by "non-team" work is illustrated in the following chart.

The vertical axis measures teamwork capability against typical stages of organizational growth measured along the horizontal axis.

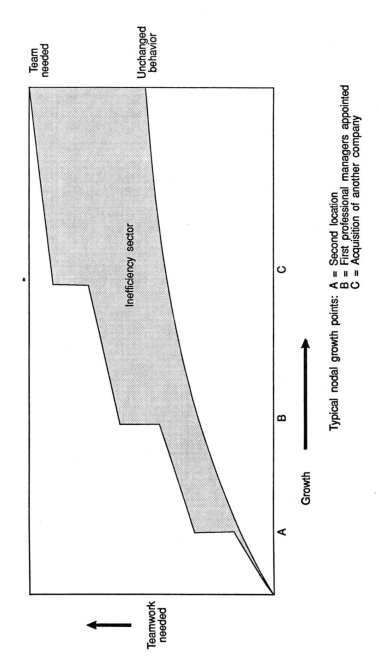

Team needed

Unchanged behavior

Inefficiency sector

Growth

Teamwork needed

Typical nodal growth points:  A = Second location
B = First professional managers appointed
C = Acquisition of another company

57

The hard line shows how teamwork becomes an increasingly dominant need, not only in terms of complexity but also of professionalism. Depending on the industry concerned, complex organization structures (and the developing need for real specialization) tend to emerge when more than one operating site is involved. As new activities (such as diversification away from a core business or significant addition to a product range) are added, control and management need to be more highly organized if a consistently acceptable result is to be achieved. These requirements are self-evident. The more interesting line is the one that defines the sector of inefficiency resulting from the involvement of the *unchanged* entrepreneur.

That line shows that an entrepreneur is an effective manager when the team is small, because his enthusiasm and leadership skills are transmitted well through short lines of communication. His colleagues work within this "aura," act flexibly, accept his idiosyncratic style without difficulty, and share a powerful vision of what the organization seeks to achieve. This missionary zeal can infect a small number of locations and a limited range of activities without any significant loss of efficiency. Successful professionals working in this environment tend to share some of the entrepreneur's anti-bureaucratic bias and consequently more readily accept the informality and lack of systems inherent in the decision-taking process. It is worth noting that the selection of these characteristics in the first professionals to join an entrepreneur is absolutely vital if a later process of acceptance of change is to follow. If the professional appointed is too rigid or systems-orientated, the mutual frustration felt by him and the entrepreneur can often lead to the development of a very unsatisfactory relationship. If it subsequently fails altogether, the entrepreneur is quite likely to claim: "I hired a qualified engineer (accountant, designer, computer expert, etc.) once—it was a disaster! I'll never make the same mistake again!" The experience encourages him to resist the appointment of another professional, however pressing and obvious the need may become as the business grows. Many potentially very successful businesses are condemned to remain small as a result of this factor alone.

As the lines of communication with the entrepreneur become longer and the need for greater formality in the management process increases, the adverse effect on efficiency of an unchanged style also increases. The problem is simple: the entrepreneur must have regular and personal contact to reinforce his influence. When absent, the opportunities for gossip, rumor, and criticism abound. He is therefore faced either with the Herculean task of regularly seeing, and being seen by, a wider and wider group of people or increasing the intensity of his occasional contacts. The latter approach usually involves powerfully articulated instructions (or sales messages) with a minimum of persuasion. For example, the owner visits the outlying subsidiary for two hours, looks over the factory, makes instant policy decisions, gives a wide variety of instructions and departs for another three months. The effects soon wear off and he seldom finds the desired result on his next visit. He then either tries again or fires a few people to set an example. Either way, he needs compliant and willing subordinates if he is going to get away with this method. High quality managers are unlikely to be attracted to or retained by companies that operate in this way.

The root cause of these problems, and of the widening inefficiency sector as the business grows, is the unwillingness of the entrepreneur to give any real authority to anyone else. Such sharing of authority and responsibility is essential for any team effort. Entrepreneurs often feel uncomfortable in teams, always wanting to lead whatever their degree of competence, and are quite capable of employing spoiling tactics if the team effort seems to be gaining too much prominence.

These characteristics are those of the unchanged entrepreneur who is often destined to enjoy a limited local stardom. The changed entrepreneur follows the line of need and hence enjoys the efficiencies of the large corporation as well as the imagination and drive of their smaller and more innovative competitors. How is it done?

## The making of the team-player

There are three components in this process of change. They can be summarized as:

1. Organizational awareness.
2. Judgments about people.
3. Self-management.

Each element has a vital role to play and all three are needed if the change is to succeed.

### Organizational awareness

The entrepreneur has to learn and consistently follow the organizational "shape" which suits him best. For example, Richard Branson insists that all his ventures are organized into small units with only a handful of senior people involved. Other entrepreneurs are more comfortable when dealing with only one individual in each major business (the entrepreneurial "echo") irrespective of how big that business is.

59

The roles of those who make commercial decisions and those who provide technical support must be sorted out in the entrepreneur's mind and a formula developed and followed. This applies, too, to the distinction between *policies* and *executive action* and level of authority appropriate for different people. It does not actually matter what the organizational form is so long as:

- It works for the entrepreneur.
- It is consistently followed.

Organizational awareness is, therefore, partly an intellectual process of inquiry and analysis into what works best, and partly the application of a degree of self-discipline to ensure that rules are followed. Experience constantly reminds one that people are more concerned about certainty than about the absolutes of the regime itself. In essence, it is better to know that you will be given one square meal a day than never to know whether or when you will be feasted or starved.

### People judgments

The second element is the conscious recognition by the entrepreneur that he must employ neither clones nor yes men, but people of real competence and character. This may seem self-evident, but the startlingly high levels of management-staff turnover in many growing entrepreneurial businesses are testament to the extent to which this is a problem. In making this change, entrepreneurs often need a lot of help, not least because they tend to be very bad interviewers. Being quick-witted and decisive people themselves, they often judge the suitability of a candidate in the first minute of an interview. For the rest of the allocated hour the interviewer will talk enthusiastically about the business while the candidate nods and murmurs occasional assent. "An excellent candidate," will be the entrepreneur's conclusion, despite his having collected no real data beyond the first spontaneous impression.

As businesses grow, so does the significance of some appointments in terms of business success or failure. Casual judgments are not only careless—they are particularly dangerous. The changing entrepreneur not only recognizes this, but is also willing to accept advice and counsel on the processes involved.

### Self-management

The most important change of all relates to a willingness on the part of the entrepreneur to reorganize his personal lifestyle. One of the greatest benefits of being your own boss is the freedom it offers the individual to do what he likes with his day. All entrepreneurs quickly realize that this is a limited freedom; the demands of the business are such that constant and effective attention to it are essential. As capable subordinates join the enterprise, the pressure eases and the potential for variety increases. Days can be spent on the golf course, exploring a business deal, or back in the office working over decisions with colleagues. The income level enjoyed by the successful man reinforces this freedom and inevitably there is a temptation for him to organize his life to suit himself and no one else.

Many small businesses are very efficiently and successfully managed on this basis. They offer a wholly satisfying life to the owners in terms of income and job satisfaction. They reflect their chosen lifestyles and make an invaluable contribution to the economy. Whether or not the owners recognize the choices they have made must be a matter of speculation. The demonstrable fact is that few, in practice, are willing and able to make the transition that is needed to the more ordered and organized life that is a prerequisite of sustained longer-term growth.

The self-disciplined entrepreneur recognizes the need for the following:

- Personal time management—the thoughtful apportionment of time to the various available activities.

- Systematic communication with key individuals, whether the group is small or large, on a sufficiently frequent basis to encourage efficient operations.

- Reliability of behavior, allowing always for the needs of a special opportunity or crisis, so that a methodical approach is supported rather than sabotaged.

- Moderation of style—difficult for many—involving the acceptance that documentation, formality, debate, and monitoring are all necessary parts of running a successful enterprise.

There is nothing here that will surprise any experienced business executive. What it represents for the fast-moving entrepreneur, however, is often an insuperable hurdle. Professional advisers frequently have a crucial, catalytic role to play in ensuring that the change is made with as much emphasis on the benefits (and conversely as little on the pain) as possible. Making money consistently and long term over a widening horizon of interests may seem easy to the entrepreneur convinced of his own abilities. In truth, it needs organization, good people, and self-discipline. The entrepreneur must grasp and deliver each if he is to succeed.

## I know best!

The process of learning to be a team-player can, and sometimes does, lead the previously successful entrepreneur down a dangerous path towards equivocation and indecision. Everyone knows the old definition of a committee as "a cul-de-sac into which ideas are lured and quietly murdered." The single-mindedness of the leader can equally be subject to the destructive forces of debate if they are allowed to get out of hand.

The need to delegate, consult, and take expert counsel must be tempered by a degree of self-confidence which at its simplest can be expressed as "I know best!" In some cases this manifests itself in a willingness to override the most compelling and logical counter-arguments—to go out on a limb and to quell adverse comment. It is perhaps the most central indication of the entrepreneur at work that he will, when convinced of the rightness of his case, follow his own judgment whatever the strength of the counter-arguments.

By saying "I know best," the entrepreneur not only personally embraces the inherent risk of failure, but also the loyalty and support of those around him. To ignore sensible advice and logical argument simply out of bravado is, of course, a sure road to failure. To assess the risks and opportunities differently from those around you and make a decision based on "gut feeling" is quite different. A practical example will illustrate the distinction.

◆   ◆   ◆

A successful operator of used car dealerships decides to expand his business into a major new urban center. The market analysis and competitor information he obtains, backed by the calculations made by his accountant, suggest that the available payback in the new territory is small and the risk of failure considerable. The forecasts suggest that not only will the market be hard to break into, it will also offer little in terms of satisfactory long-term results. The owner decides to go ahead anyway, and after months of hard work and losses decides to close down the new outlet. The reasons for the failure were exactly those described in the initial analysis: the operator failed to find any new "angle" or exploitable opportunity that would prove that analysis fallacious. The process of being proved right no doubt please the professionals, but was costly in terms of both finance and reputation to the entrepreneur himself.

Contrast this case with that of a manufacturer bringing a new form of packaging material to the grocery trade. Experimental operations have demonstrated the superior qualities of the new material and its potentially very advantageous cost characteristics. There is only one snag—the plant needed to manufacture significant volumes requires a very large capital investment and the payback is highly speculative in view of the novelty of the material. Conventional analysis, based on the rate of uptake of comparable new products, suggests that the risks are unacceptably high and rejection of the project or, at best, a joint venture with a major corporation is universally recommended. The entrepreneur says, "I know best," and presses on to bring the project to a startlingly successful launch and equally profitable further development phase.

◆   ◆   ◆

Why was this a different result from the earlier example? The reason is that the first entrepreneur failed to find any new way to sell cars; the second, by contrast, showed a special insight into the behavior of manufacturers of grocery products. He realized that the attraction of the packaging material to the manufacturer lay not only in its lower cost, but also in its ability to display the product more effectively on the shelf. This intangible benefit was "felt" by the promoter of the project rather than measured in any conventional way. In prospect, he saw this factor in terms of specific levels of sales and manufacturing potential, which made him more inherently optimistic than any of the forecasts. More optimistic but not groundlessly so—hence the key difference between the examples.

Many of these moments of judgment are as instinctive and difficult to analyze as the ones described above, although a "hunch" or "feel" are seldom as irrational as they might at first appear. Many entrepreneurs claim to rely on little else although, in truth, the combination of shrewd observation, fine judgment of risk, and a facility with numbers is seldom easy to describe. An entrepreneur unable (or unwilling) to make controversial decisions is likely to be a long-term loser. He is allowed and expected to make mistakes, and many would argue that, without failure, the individual is ill-prepared to achieve long-term success. Clearly, the stronger the track record the more robust the capability to sustain a particular setback, whether as a result of an "I know best" decision or a fully supported analysis. The most valuable insight an entrepreneur can have, however, is the ability to know just why he contradicts opposing advice when his decision ultimately proves the right one. Armed with that knowledge, he should be able to go anywhere!

## Summary

The entrepreneur is an easily recognizable and undoubted individualist. The distinctive characteristics are an invariable propensity to rebel and an impatience with the conventional. Although various theories have been advanced to explain this, the underlying reason is likely to be his desire for recognition and "applause."

As a non-joiner, the entrepreneur rarely makes a good team member. Although this is potentially an advantage when a business is small, it increasingly affects efficiency as it grows. If the entrepreneur is unwilling or unable to change, this can determine the scope for growth more certainly than any other factor. To achieve the change from a non-team player to a team-player he needs to learn new skills and attitudes, not least in terms of how he organizes his own business life.

An entrepreneur must be able to stamp his authority on key decisions even if his view appears to fly in the face of logical analysis and advice. The "hunch" factor is often based on clear, but subconscious, processes that are extremely valid in relation to the commercial argument. The entrepreneur who can rationalize this capability and turn it to work for him has a remarkable and powerful tool at his command.

*Chapter 5*

# Manager

A crucial element in the make-up of the successful entrepreneur, in addition to his being an innovator and a risk-taker, is his role as a manager. The management process he uses is usually very different from that normally associated with established businesses. In this chapter we explore some of the characteristics of the entrepreneur in performing the essential tasks needed to follow through from the inception of the business idea to its realization as a profitable enterprise.

## Opportunist or planner?
The following table is drawn from the March-April 1985 edition of the *Harvard Business Review*. In the article "The Heart of Entrepreneurship", Howard Stevenson and David Gumpert drew a series of contrasting pictures of the entrepreneurial versus the administrative culture. The table overleaf summarizes the characteristics and pressures of the extremes of an entrepreneurial focus and an administrative focus. Its significance for the entrepreneur lies in the insight it offers into the management culture in which they thrive, compared with those dedicated to more bureaucratic objectives.

Each of the cultural dimensions is worth a brief commentary.

# The entrepreneurial culture vs. the administrative culture

*Entrepreneurial focus*

|  | Characteristics | Pressures |
|---|---|---|
| **A**<br>**Strategic**<br>**orientation** | Driven by perception of opportunity | Diminishing opportunities<br><br>Rapidly changing technology, consumer economics, social values and political rules |
| **B**<br>**Commitment**<br>**to seize**<br>**opportunities** | Revolutionary, with short duration | Action orientation<br><br>Narrow decision windows<br><br>Acceptance of reasonable risks<br><br>Few decision constituencies |
| **C**<br>**Commitment**<br>**of resources** | Many stages, with minimal exposure at each stage | Lack of predictable resource needs<br><br>Lack of control over the environment<br><br>Social demands for appropriate use of resources<br><br>Foreign competition<br><br>Demands for more efficient resource use |
| **D**<br>**Control of**<br>**resources** | Episodic use or rent of required resources | Increased resource specialization<br><br>Long resource life compared with need<br><br>Risk of obsolescence<br><br>Risk inherent in the identified opportunity<br><br>Inflexibility of permanent commitment to resources |
| **E**<br>**Management**<br>**structure** | Flat, with multiple informal networks | Coordination of key non-controlled resources<br><br>Challenge to hierarchy<br><br>Employees' desire for independence |

| Characteristics | Pressures |
| --- | --- |
| Driven by controlled resources | Social contracts |
| | Performance measurement criteria |
| | Planning systems and cycles |
| Evolutionary, with long duration | Acknowledgment of multiple constituencies |
| | Negotiation about strategic course |
| | Risk reduction |
| | Coordination with existing resource base |
| A single stage, with complete commitment resulting from a decision | Need to reduce risk |
| | Incentive compensation |
| | Turnover in managers |
| | Capital budgeting systems |
| | Formal planning systems |
| Ownership or employment of required resources | Power, status and financial rewards |
| | Coordination of activity |
| | Efficiency measures |
| | Inertia and cost of change |
| | Industry structures |
| Hierarchy | Need for clearly defined authority and responsibility |
| | Organizational culture |
| | Reward systems |
| | Management theory |

### Strategic vision

The entrepreneur feels the pressure of a changing world and the need to grasp opportunities by the scruff of the neck. The bureaucrat, by contrast, feels the pressure to demonstrate his control of his business environment and sees this as a desirable strategic objective. Thus, the two see the world in a totally different light: the entrepreneur sees energetic exploitation as a desirable goal while the bureaucrat is cautious and conservative. This analysis also suggests that there is a time pressure on the entrepreneur evidenced by a feeling that unless he acts quickly the window of opportunity will close. Bureaucrats, by contrast, are more concerned with method than with output and assume a relatively unchanged external environment.

### Seizing opportunities

The entrepreneur wants to get on with the job, and his actions are decision-orientated. He therefore consults few people in the process and relies strongly on his own judgment. The administrator, by contrast, uses more incremental processes based on wider consultation and negotiation. He is aware of the existing situation and seeks to amend and develop it without involving radical change. Once again, the entrepreneur is more aware of time pressure than his bureaucratic counterpart.

### Resource commitment

The pressures illustrated as applying to the entrepreneur have in common a rather chaotic state of interacting forces, with the entrepreneur sitting at the center. His approach is eclectic, consisting of picking off each element of the equation and dealing with it individually. By contrast, the administrator sees the need for a homogeneous pattern of interlocking systems and methods that will integrate with decision-taking processes. These show a clear contrast between recognition of a chaotic world from which order can seldom be expected on the one hand and an ordered world in which chaos is an aberration on the other. The entrepreneur often seeks to exploit chaos while the bureaucrat strives to bring it into order. This analysis of extremes does not bring out the fact that the entrepreneur's approach to resource commitment is usually no less systematic than that of the administrator; it simply has a different point of departure in terms of the assumptions made about the environment in which each must work.

## Resource control

The entrepreneurial focus is on an opportunity driven commitment to resources, to the point of a careless lack of concern for the longer term. By contrast, the bureaucrat is anxiously concerned for the efficiency and coordination of resources and is deeply conscious of their long-term effectiveness. This suggests that the entrepreneur is more interested in the *output* of the process, namely profit, than in the means of achieving it. "Control" as an activity is, therefore, inherently uninteresting unless it has a very direct and evident bearing on the outcome of the venture.

## Management structure

The entrepreneur classically uses very informal and direct lines of management in the control of his business activities. By contrast, the administrator seeks clarity of organization and hierarchy as a means of achieving control over the enterprise. The entrepreneur, therefore, acts to harness management effort towards the achievement of a well-articulated and common goal, whereas the bureaucrat seeks to make the individual the servant of the system.

The two models described in the table represent extreme by readily recognizable descriptions of the way entrepreneurs, as distinct from bureaucrats, behave. Both styles of management are valid and effective in their respective environments. It is important, however, to recognize that the entrepreneur manages his business in a very different way from his opposite number in a more conventional and mature organization. Thus, he is likely to be more concerned with the achievement of short-term objectives, more profligate with resources, and less sensitive to the need for structure and consultation than his more professionally trained colleague. This can be illustrated by a real-life example.

◆　◆　◆

A successful businessman, Harry Wren, runs three clothing factories making ladies' fashion garments. The three factories are within ten miles of one another and employ some 150 full-time staff plus 300 part-time outworkers. One factory manufactures skirts, another jackets, and the third slacks. Harry manages the factories through a constant round of personal supervision at each location, which he combines with visiting major customers, choosing each season's designs, and buying key raw materials. His investment in equipment is substantial, and he prides himself on the efficiency of his manufacturing facilities.

One day he is approached by a potential major customer. This large chain of retailers has grown dissatisfied with their existing supplier and is contemplating a change. The total order they could offer Harry would represent 80 percent of his annual output, but would involve scrapping a major part of his existing plan. His business would become "tied" to one customer, although the opportunity for long-term profit looks very attractive.

Harry conceives the notion that he can exploit this business opportunity by combining two of his existing units and adding a major new production facility, all of which would be located on an out-of-town site. This project involves a considerable gamble in terms of loss of production continuity, the willingness of his labor force to relocate, and the potential payback on a substantial investment in new plant. Harry's exercise in planning involves a relatively optimistic view of each of these factors. He is sanguine about his capability to serve his new customer long term and, indeed, expand the business further on the basis of the connection.

In the end, Harry's plan foundered through lack of appreciation of the practical difficulties involved in making a complex change to his business. The individualistic, hands-on style which had proved so successful was quite inadequate to cope with the logistics of a major operation. His management and planning processes were too weak to avoid a disastrous failure in producing the quantities and quality required. As a result, Harry was left with a major investment burden and a very dissatisfied customer, waiting for the first opportunity to move elsewhere. Harry then had little option but to retrench and adopt more conventional management processes to help him out of his difficulty.

◆　　◆　　◆

There are many illustrations of how the informality and opportunism of the entrepreneur contribute to the successful early growth of young organizations. In these early phases, the entrepreneur not only has an encyclopedic knowledge of his business and all that goes on in it, but also a keenness to attend to detail that in some cases verges on the paranoic. Such individuals have been known to fly into a rage if some small aspect of a sales presentation or a letter fails to meet his personal quality expectations. A misplaced desk in an office, an untidy showroom, or a badly typed address on a letter can each offend the entrepreneur's perfectionism. The instant dismissal of a badly dressed clerk by a bad-tempered entrepreneur is certainly not unknown.

This understanding of the business and attention to detail weakens as the business grows. The entrepreneur attempts to compensate by both working harder and relying on spot checks. His grasp of details of the company's affairs inexorably weakens, and, in consequence, he must rely increasingly on the work of his managers and subordinates. They have been used to a boss with a total grasp of the business, and have probably had little authority or decision-taking responsibility. The owner's need to delegate may, therefore, not find a response in the capability of his subordinates. They may have become too set in their ways to change or simply lack the talent to grow with the business. For the reasons described earlier in this chapter, the entrepreneur is sometimes the last person to introduce and manage essential new systems and, as a result, the growth process slows and ultimately stops.

A well-organized entrepreneur recognizes that he faces a series of watershed decision points at which his willingness to adjust the focus of the organization is called into question.

## Typical watershed decision points

There are a number of these inherent in the growth of most entrepreneurial businesses. The following are some illustrations:

- The need for costing and management reporting systems other than the checkbook or the back of the entrepreneur's personal envelope.
- The need to define the job responsibilities of senior colleagues and their working relationships to each other.
- The introduction, for the first time, of a senior professionally trained manager.
- The need to be accountable to some third party, such as a minority shareholder or banker.
- Becoming involved in a joint venture or trading for the first time overseas.
- The acquisition of another company, particularly when it trades in a different location or product range.

The "correct" response at these decision points will inevitably vary depending on the particular circumstances of the company in terms of size, profitability and business sector. There will, however, always be a need to move towards formality and a more systematic method of management. The challenge for the entrepreneur is to adapt to these needs without sacrificing the essential qualities which have made his business successful up to that time.

## Retaining the good qualities

The paradox of the managerial behavior of the entrepreneur is the apparent ease with which a careless disregard for conventional management methods is often combined with extraordinary efficiency of operation. There can be no doubt that the overall orientation of a small business can give it a distinct competitive advantage over its more hierarchically structured and ponderous competitors. The boundaries that normally exist between separate jobs disappear in a strongly motivated small team. The catalytic effect of a focused and energetic owner serves to encourage people both to care about their working responsibilities and to perform above their normal potentiality. The adrenaline charge which accompanies a high-risk business venture is perhaps akin to that experienced by the soldier in combat. The entrepreneur both understands and exploits this emotional drive.

In conditions of aggressive leadership, the entrepreneur's judgment and instructions are seldom questioned. For example, if he takes extraordinary steps to check on the fine details of subordinates' actions it is likely to be interpreted as caring for the overall performance of the enterprise as much as unwelcome interference in it. One owner of a successful engineering company saw every incoming and outgoing piece of correspondence, even when the annual turnover amounted to $20 million. Another insisted on personally checking the layout of every branch office in a national network and adjusting the seating arrangements to his personal taste. A successful business owner who personally checks every employee's expense claim is not uncommon.

This very personal and involved style is frequently combined with an unconventional approach to business management. Some typical traits of behavior are:

- Great impatience with any sort of formal meeting.
- A dislike of routine as exemplified by regular management information in all its forms.
- An unwillingness to define individuals' roles with particular clarity or to treat them consistently.
- A demonstrating his command of the decision-making structure by periodically upsetting it without apparent cause.

It would be foolish to suggest that many successful entrepreneurs do not develop into highly capable managers. However, they often seem to retain some, if not all, of the characteristics listed above, if only in a more muted and controlled form.

A management style that has a shifting focus has some distinct advantages. Thus the entrepreneur who brings to his boardroom a particular concern for intensive debate and discussion, sweeping aside the normal agenda, may achieve more than is possible in the structured environment of a larger company. For example, if the owner becomes obsessed with the idea of selling the company's product in Europe, he might introduce it unheralded at a board meeting and insist on its being fully debated there and then. This often irritates and frustrates functionally responsible directors who would have preferred thinking and preparation time before making a reasoned submission. The element of surprise, however, often leads to more successful brainstorming than weeks of careful preparation. Many entrepreneurs consciously employ this tactic to develop an important issue without being pressed to make a particular decision; it often adds to their capability of acting quickly and opportunistically. The difficulty experienced executives have in adapting to this style of environment should not, however, be underrated. A sales or finance director joining a rapidly growing company from a larger enterprise will often find this highly volatile management approach very difficult to cope with. As one senior director put it, "It's like a combination of a roller coaster and the tunnel of love. It is enormously exciting and confusing at one and the same time. I quickly gave up trying to find my organizational bearings and let myself be swept along by the tide of the company's enthusiasm."

## Non-planning

Since the essence of entrepreneurship is the quickness of wit to seize commercial opportunities and to innovate, it is, theoretically at least, counter to the planning ethic. As discussed earlier, entrepreneurs can demonstrate considerable accomplishment when it comes to planning where the persuasion of others is the prime purpose. Thus the fundraising stage in any major venture must involve a considerable degree of care in preparing forecasts if it is to prove successful. This style of planning, which attempts to describe and predict future events, is much more agreeable to the entrepreneur than the formalized system used for day-to-day management purposes. Skills in the use of budgetary control and cash-flow forecasting are not those that immediately come to mind when considering the successful entrepreneur. There are, of course, notable exceptions, particularly in such fields as property development, commodity trading, international banking, and finance. By and large, the entrepreneur gets bored with such mundane management tools, and while he is fully prepared to allow others to employ them if they wish, he seldom feels the obligation to be constrained by them himself.

Presenting a business proposition to an entrepreneur also requires special skills. The concept, the market opportunity, and the vision of what can be achieved are as important as the detailed financial projections. The overall result must, of course, be clearly explained and risks and return closely argued. Adding a venture to the portfolio of an entrepreneur is a more subtle process than simply offering him a money-making opportunity. The venture has implications for his personal standing, his business power base and the opportunities for future leverage. These must be fully taken into account when judging the likely reaction to what may seem a particularly attractive deal.

## A sound judge of people
The non-planning entrepreneur must of necessity rely very heavily on the support and energy of his management team. As businesses develop and grow, his reliance on such individuals increases enormously. He must therefore:

- Choose them carefully.
- Use them effectively.
- Maintain the strength of the team.

### Successful choices
Choosing able lieutenants, particularly when they operate in specialized areas, is a very difficult job for the inexperienced businessman. He tends to look for a combination of personal and professional qualities that are often very difficult to find, particularly in those who are willing to take the chance of working for a headstrong boss. The personal qualities seem to require a subordinate to be strong and independent-minded, but only to the point at which compliance with the ultimate decision of the entrepreneur is both accepted and implemented. It is flattering to the entrepreneur to engage in stimulating internal debate with the confident knowledge that his final judgment will prevail. Many with a modest educational background seek out those with some academic distinction and take pride in the reflected glory of their achievement. In reality the employee, if he survives, comes to recognize the nature of the trade-off and seeks compensation for it through the salary or dividend check. Entrepreneurs prefer their colleagues to be good listeners and to be able to conjure up the necessary enthusiasm for the company mission. They are expected to be loyal and not prone

to conspiracy; they are also assumed to be willing to give little priority to their private lives when the demands of the company dictate otherwise.

In technical disciplines, the entrepreneur is often on much weaker ground. He may find it extremely difficult to judge the competence of an individual despite an apparently illustrious track record. The informality of the management style often means that an individual's inadequacy takes a long time to be revealed. The appointment of the very first finance director, for example, may attract to a company an individual with a wholly unsuitable background. He may be more interested in doing deals with the owner than in managing a well-organized accounts department. The entrepreneur's lack of technical understanding of the issues involved along with no formal system of review may leave this problem unappreciated until some collapse occurs. Similar examples would apply in the manufacturing and technical areas of a business, although the entrepreneur usually has a better understanding of products and processes than he does of finance. Some managers undoubtedly enjoy the freedom of informality of the less strictly structured entrepreneurial business environment; they can be both more creative and influential in its development. It is also a more precarious position to be in.

### Effective personnel management

Typically, the entrepreneur communicates with his managers orally rather than in writing and with no particular, regular agenda. The communication process is therefore characterized by an untidy melange of major and minor items handled in no ordered sequence of logic or priority. The sales director, for example, might speak to his boss four times in the course of a day. The issues might be:

- Pricing a major new contract for which a tender is due to be submitted.

- A complaint about late delivery from a customer whom the owner has met casually at lunch-time.

- Sales commission levels for the coming year.

- A hotel bill for a salesman's stay abroad, attached to a check requiring the owner's signature.

This typical kaleidoscopic pattern of day-to-day interchange involves little in the form of direct instruction or formal performance review and monitoring. The executive must use each contact with the owner as another small piece of evidence in the jigsaw of his job role. This may itself represent a moving picture as the entrepreneur explores the boundaries of his subordinate's contribution to the business.

Few entrepreneurs comply with the common image of the autocrat barking instructions down the phone to his trembling subordinate. The style is much more likely to be indirect and persuasive, particularly when senior colleagues are involved. For example, one most feared entrepreneur never seemed to give a direct instruction. He would say, "George, maybe you should check out the results of the Boston branch," or, "I was wondering, Frank, if the sales figures for the last quarter really came up to your expectations," and so on. The message behind the innocent comment or question was entirely clear to his colleagues and energetic action invariably followed.

The utterances of some entrepreneurs are more Delphic and are probably aimed at keeping the management team on its toes. Thus an entrepreneur might comment to his board, "I'm pretty unhappy about the way our business is organized," without any further explanation. The effect on individuals can, of course, be galvanizing since no one is sure at whom the remark is directed. Another technique is the so-called "confidential briefing" of one colleague about another with a high degree of certainty that the information will leak to the person about whom the comment is made. Demanding, and usually receiving, considerable personal loyalty from his subordinates does not always earn the corresponding response from the entrepreneur: as companies grow, the business management team forms "clusters" of professionalism at some remove from the influence of the entrepreneur himself. They may be very formally structured, as would be the case in a conventional company owned at arm's length by a successful man. Part of that function is to "translate" and, on occasion, rationalize the entrepreneur's decisions. The owner would communicate with key people at board level and they would be subject to his particular style, however idiosyncratic. However, lower levels of operational management would be insulated from this influence.

Despite these apparent flaws, entrepreneurs are frequently very skillful in wresting high-level performance out of their immediate subordinates. The word "charisma" is often used to describe the special quality which these natural leaders possess. It is difficult to describe in simple terms, but is often instantly recognizable when someone who possesses it enters the room. It is partly the reputation of the individual that is subconsciously transmitted to those around him; it is also partly the exceptional commitment and energy some people bring to all their activities. This yields an almost involuntary recognition in most of us, and goes some way to explaining why the professional manager is often willing to work in what others might regard as very unsatisfactory business circumstances.

## A healthy team

Entrepreneurs are commonly seen to be, and indeed are, extremely ruthless when it comes to dealing with individuals. Issues of fairness are often subordinated to the interest of the enterprise or the entrepreneur himself. In many cases, the attitude towards an individual colleague is less than wholly rational, and the more senior his position the more vulnerable he is likely to be. Typical causes of an unheralded dismissal at this level include:

- Suspicion of disloyalty or conspiracy.
- A fall from favor, perhaps over some apparently trifling point or issue.
- A major confrontation which goes beyond the boundaries of the unwritten protocol between the two individuals.
- Boredom and a wish for change.

These reasons may appear facile at first glance, but must be taken seriously by the senior executive who values the security of his position. Conventional assumptions about the gentlemanly conduct of one individual to another, particularly when the association is a long-standing one, tend to prove unreliable. The entrepreneur's actions are often sudden and brutal, but financially generous. It seems almost as if his mind can flick over from a lively and highly personal association one day to a cold independence the next; the actions are justified by what is seen to be the better interest of the business itself. A reputation for being decisive in handling people can be an entrepreneur's strong card and the occasional senior management dismissal can *encourage les autres.* In private, the entrepreneur often finds the process both distasteful and difficult and suffers many of the anxieties which would be expected of more feeling individuals. These anxieties are never displayed in public for much the same reason that a successful military commander would not reveal to his troops his doubts about the potential success of a campaign. In many cases, the "hard but fair" philosophy is a valuable component in the entrepreneurial style.

Many large companies suffer from a reluctance to make difficult decisions. They often tend to dodge the issue either by compromising the process of judgment itself or shying away from the unpleasantness of a personal confrontation. The shake-out in British industry in the early 1980s hardened many managers' attitudes towards this problem.

Despite this, there is still a general tendency for companies to become increasingly bureaucratic and impersonal as they grow, with a resultant blurring of the sharp edges of personal assessment so important for the entrepreneur.

Healthy teams exist in all types of organizations. They are often, however, no more than a fleeting phenomenon, and it requires a firm hand and keen judgment to maintain their effectiveness. Military history indicates the frequency with which generals need to change their command teams for continued success in the field. The analogy applies equally well to the business world. Using the military parallel, the entrepreneur has an understanding of the objectives of the campaign and consequently thinks little of the changes he needs to make in his senior team to achieve success. Some large organizations are sufficiently astute to recognize the need constantly to reiterate such a strategic vision. They rarely succeed in maintaining a healthy team, however, unless they are prepared to apply a similar degree of entrepreneurial ruthlessness to it.

## The ethics of management

It is often argued that entrepreneurs find it difficult to distinguish between management behavior which is generally acceptable (or "ethical") and that which falls into a more dubious category. The interesting issue here is not one of the entrepreneur acting illegally (for which there are clear risks and penalties); it is rather the question of why such people are so commonly assumed to act in a relatively underhanded way and whether this assumption is valid.

Given that entrepreneurs are frequently unconventional and untrained, at least in the early stages of their careers, it is hardly surprising that they do not conform to common management stereotypes. Someone working with an entrepreneur is likely to see only a fraction of his total working methods. As entrepreneurs are individualistic, and often secretive in their approach, this "glimpse" of how the boss works can be disturbing for more conventionally trained managers. Decision-making can appear sporadic and partial if not occasionally contradictory, and since the entrepreneur collects data from many sources but often keeps his own counsel, his methods can give rise to suspicions of conspiracy. However much his success is recognized and applauded, his motives may be questioned. His attempts to communicate and explain his actions frequently create the reverse of the desired effect among his colleagues. Thus, the wish to rationalize and explain a process which is essentially somewhat arcane does no more than ring new alarm bells.

All these factors tend to create an atmosphere in which assumptions of deviousness flourish. These are further reinforced by typical questions about what rules are normal and how far they can be broken within the boundaries of legality. Accountants and lawyers are very familiar with such questions from their entrepreneurial clients. For example, an entrepreneur in the process of bidding for a private company owned by a widely spread family may ask how far it is usual to approach distant relatives at the same time as dealing with the major shareholder. He might be told that such a method is legal but generally regarded as unethical, since such negotiations are dealt with through principal shareholders whose views are respected in such situations. The entrepreneur may or may not seek to ignore the ethical rules, but by asking the question he is showing an inclination to be, at best, unconventional in his methods.

It can be argued that the entrepreneur is a valuable catalyst in the process of change, continually throwing down challenges to the conventional order. When Sir Charles Clore of the British Shoe Corporation first started the process of buying and breaking up companies in the 1960s, his activities were regarded as deeply shocking by the financial world. Such behavior was seen as unacceptable by those brought up to expect a more gentlemanly way of doing business. However, it did not take long for the financial world to realize and accept the commanding underlying logic of the Clore method. What was seen initially as a maverick approach became commonplace in later years. It is interesting to see how today's "corporate raiders" are retracing the path trodden by such original entrepreneurial minds some 30 years ago.

It is equally true to suppose that the entrepreneur feels driven by his ambition to succeed and make money to adopt whatever techniques are legally available to him. This propensity to seek a competitive advantage at any cost often makes such individuals, in prospect at least, unattractive business associates. The reputation for sharp practice often precedes that of business achievement; it has undesirable overtones and creates an atmosphere of suspicion and distrust.

In many cases, this assumption that entrepreneurs invariably sail close to the wind is quite unfounded. Being a quick and ruthless decision-maker does not necessarily mean that rules have to be broken, and a strong sense of personal ambition does not necessarily imply that the means will justify the end. In practice, there seems to be a greater likelihood of the successful entrepreneur's acting unconventionally than unethically. A case history illustrates this point.

◆　　◆　　◆

A strongly led software house is desperate to win a major systems development contract. The customer is a major public corporation, and competitors for the work have apparently much strong credentials in terms of previous relevant experience. Within the confines of legality the software house can act unethically or unconventionally. In the former category would fall, for example, head-hunting staff from competitor firms and hoping to obtain information on the rival bids during the interview process; in the latter would be creative and unusual sales techniques—for example, arranging a surprise personal demonstration of their software to the potential customer's chairman at his golf club would be unconventional but certainly not unethical. The software house concerned is more likely to adopt the latter approach than the former, and this is true of general entrepreneurial behavior. The entrepreneur's wish to be seen as a somewhat macho figure often encourages him to play to the audience: thus, he will suggest that he has obtained some information by devious means, when in reality it is available from some commonplace source. This is not to suggest that he will not exploit some loophole in law or accepted conventions, but rather that there is usually a stronger moral and ethical sense at work that popular prejudice would suggest.

◆　　◆　　◆

## Unsafe assumptions

Most businessmen and professionals rely on an unspoken but generally understood code of business practice. Their training and development lead them to make certain assumptions about the way in which others with whom they deal are likely to behave. These even extend to the minutiae of business relations, such as how people will dress, how correspondence is conducted, telephone calls are answered, and meetings are run. Entrepreneurs quite commonly have different but consistent sets of business values. For example, some entrepreneurs dispense with what are generally regarded as the courtesies of business life: correspondence remains unanswered, but meetings can be and are interrupted at his whim; colleagues and advisors are called at any time of the day or night to discuss a problem and social niceties are ignored. Everything is secondary to the immediacy of the business issue and those who work with an entrepreneur of this type must recognize and understand this priority.

Almost every entrepreneur has some idiosyncratic characteristics which make him an unconventional manager. The important message for those dealing with him is to understand his pattern of behavior and not to make any generalized assumptions based on ordinary experience. Entrepreneurs dislike being taken for granted almost as much as they dislike being ignored

## Older and wiser?

The picture that emerges from this analysis is of the entrepreneur as a dominant and individualistic manager. He has little use for management theory and imposes his own personal style on all his activities. In principle, this approach ought to impose severe limitations on the size of the enterprise such a person can control. This should be dictated by the degree to which he needs to understand the detailed issues in order to make effective decisions; beyond a certain point, there is simply insufficient time for him to make sound judgments and the success of the business is thus compromised. Depending on the type of business involved, this boundary condition would conventionally be met when more than, say, 200 people are employed.

If this were universally true, entrepreneurs would never progress beyond the confines of the small company. Indeed, many are destined to remain leaders of such businesses simply because they cannot make the transition from a "hands-on" style to a more professional management approach. For many, experience brings the necessary insight into the process of delegation and the need for more formal methods of management.

The entrepreneur also realizes that the most secure and important resource is how own time and that it must be used wisely. The personal agenda increasingly reflects self-discipline and a more ordered approach to his dealings with his colleagues; the self-indulgence that characterizes the early stages of many entrepreneurially based businesses gives way to a more conventional and ordered life. The pace and excitement may remain the same but the working structure progressively develops into a more ordered model.

Growing older and wiser may also be characterized by a more mature and measured personal style. Although there are notable exceptions to this rule, those who break through the size barrier do so, in part, by acquiring greater skills of diplomacy and professionalism. They become more reasonable, tactful and thoughtful. Their management style becomes more relaxed and considered, while remaining authoritative. In many senses, they enjoy the best of both worlds—the pleasures and wealth of the entrepreneur and the professionalism of the experienced manager.

The experience that leads some entrepreneurs but not others to realize the importance of these factors is not itself a function of age—

the lessons can be learned at a very early age and a fully-fledged "entrepreneur-manager" can emerge in his early twenties. Some achieve this breakthrough much later, perhaps as a result of learning from a series of disappointments and failures or from the experience of their peers. In private business, there are regular examples of entrepreneurs whose willingness to change their approach comes only with middle age.

None of the managerial characteristics described above is of any value without the essential flair and innovation that go with the entrepreneurial spirit. The sad truth is that success and the wealth and power that accompany it often blind the entrepreneur to the necessity for personal development if there are to be longer-term achievements. The learning process is less an intellectual exercise than one that follows an insight into enlightened self-interest. Entrepreneurs are often so convinced of their uniqueness that they find such insights difficult to accept. They are, however, ultimately the determinant of management success in the large company area.

## Summary

The entrepreneur needs to succeed as a manager if he is to achieve his goal of wealth creation and power. Management through conventional processes is not usually the entrepreneur's forte; however, he brings to the task a clear and determined style, which frequently achieves greater success than the more structured and measured methods used by larger companies. He is more likely to be unconventional than unethical in his approach to business but relishes the reputation of being troublesome. To succeed in building a business of real substance, he must learn to make the transition from a dominating and idiosyncratic style to one which involves more delegation and personal self-discipline. In the last analysis, the entrepreneur-manager will only succeed if he realizes the imperative of recognizing the contribution others can make to this ultimate achievement.

*Chapter 6*

# Prima Donna

## The Napoleon factor

An essential part of the make-up of any leader is his capacity to command the respect of his subordinates. The personal qualities involved are not easily defined, but certainly include the ability to make sound judgments about both situations and people. The skills needed to judge situations, whether at a strategic or tactical level, can be acquired by anyone with a reasonable intellectual capacity, and the armed forces and big business have demonstrated the value of investing in management training to develop their leaders, whether in the field of battle or the boardrooms. The skills needed to judge people soundly, however, are much less easily taught: although certain ground rules are generally applicable, it is clear that experience is the dominant tutor.

In conventional environment, individuals with leadership qualities are nurtured through a combination of training and front-line experience. The former broadens the intellectual horizons and introduces the analytical and planning techniques need to appraise a problem, while the latter develops the recipient's talents in the judgment of how individuals are likely to behave in differing situations. How different is this structured and progressive approach from the background experience of most entrepreneurs? Though some do, of course, emerge from backgrounds in large corporations to break away and establish new enterprises, they represent a small minority of the entrepreneurial population. Most entrepreneurs therefore emerge from backgrounds which are much less structured and hierarchical than those in which leadership skills are commonly developed. Theirs is the advantage of having an earlier, self-determined opportunity to put their leadership talents to the test; they may also have the disadvantage of lack of experience of working in a well-ordered environment that brings a different perspective to both achievements and personal standards. As already discussed, most entrepreneurs are, by their nature, non-joiners and nonconformists. Their self-belief is so strong that they set their own standards of behavior, which are frequently very different from those of the people around them. As a consequence, the entrepreneur works within his own set of standards rather than those imposed by others. The potential for him to act irrationally, unfairly, or even despotically is thereby hugely increased.

These characteristics can conveniently be called the "Napoleon factor." Some entrepreneurs, like Napoleon, suffer from such a degree of self-delusion about their own powers that they fail to anticipate, and hence to avoid, ultimate failure. They overstep the fine line between soundly judged self-confidence and reckless bravura. In extreme cases, the entrepreneur's behavior breaks the bonds of confidence which he has so carefully established with those around him and his impending failure is signalled by a collapse of the team on whose support he could previously rely. The deserted entrepreneur is left as a rather pitiable figure proclaiming his mastery of a situation no longer his to command.

It seems that all entrepreneurs have the potential to cross this line and hence considerably increase the risk of failure. It is therefore instructive both to them and to those around them to be aware of the early symptoms of a possible problem. There are three critical indicators:

- The demand for loyalty.
- The uncertain temper.
- Unreliable leadership.

**The demand for loyalty**
The trail-blazing entrepreneur creates loyalty through the dedication he has to his project and his ability to convert opportunity into profit. The loyalty this creates is founded perhaps more in admiration for an extraordinary talent than respect for the personal qualities of the entrepreneur. In these early stages, the entrepreneur is more likely to persuade and lead by example than by direction and command. As success is achieved, the influence of the entrepreneur, particularly over his subordinates, increases rapidly and can extend far beyond what appears to an independent observer as wholly rational. This situation can be illustrated by a simple, real life example.

◆　　◆　　◆

Freddie Jones, at 50, is a successful entrepreneur. Having founded a building company in his twenties, he now owns three hotels and a travel agency and has gathered around him a professional management team including a finance director. His leisure-time passion is sailing and he can see a new business venture in the boat-building business. All his advisors, including his own management, strongly advise that it would be very unwise to go ahead with this investment. They point out the rate of business failures in that sector, the overcapacity already available in the industry and the difficulties inherent in controlling boat-building staff. Despite the advice, Freddie pursues his instinct, buys the boatyard and proceeds to invest heavily in it. The funds needed considerably exceed original estimates. Freddie has to borrow against his other investments and then, after 18 months, sell some of his assets to keep the project going. His originally cheerful forecast of a highly successful and profitable business are gradually replaced by an expectation of break-even and then loss minimization. Ultimately, he is forced to close the boatyard, lay off workers, and sell the stock for whatever it will realize.

◆　　◆　　◆

This sad episode extends over a total period of three years. The enterprise was entirely at the risk of Freddie himself and this was recognized by his boardroom colleagues. After the initial commitment was made, however, Freddie would not permit any of them, at any time, to make comments suggesting that the original judgment was at fault. The problems and the loss-making were attributed to "the market" or "labor relations" or "poor on-site management." He expected, and got, an extraordinary degree of public loyalty from his colleagues. In private, of course, they were endlessly critical of the decision and the absurd tenaciousness with which Freddie followed it through. His demand for unquestioning loyalty to his business judgment silenced relevant and sound criticism. Freddie believed that he had an open and frank relationship with his colleagues. He was quite unaware of the perfectly understandable reticence on their part to question his judgment once the decision had been made. He had demanded a degree of loyalty from them, quite subconsciously, that they were willing to give because the risk was not theirs. This brought an air of unreality to the boardroom and distanced the entrepreneur from what had previously been a closely knit team of colleagues.

Chastened by the experience of the boatyard and an accidental report to the effect the venture had had on the confidence of his colleagues, Freddie decided to put the record straight. He sought an independent and totally frank assessment of the business venture and made sure that the findings were circulated to his colleagues. In discussing these findings with them, he castigated them for what he saw as their "conspiracy of silence" and was self-critical of his assumption of their loyalty towards him. The accusation that the management team had conspired against him was clearly unfair, but, once out in the open, revealed to Freddie the true nature of his dominant relationship over them and what needed to be done to restore open frank communication in the future. The team spirit was re-established and the danger of another failure considerably reduced.

This example deals with a major business venture. The entrepreneur's demand for loyalty is often also evident when small issues are involved. He expects people to see his point of view in relatively trivial matters and his subordinates may opt for a quiet life rather than run the risk of a damaging confrontation. Once in the habit of exerting a powerful influence in small issues, the executive can find himself taking a similar approach to more weighty matters. This is a slippery slope both for the entrepreneur himself and the individual reporting to him: all successful businessmen need sounding boards for their ideas, and a strong and well-informed management team is the best place to start. If the entrepreneur has got into the habit of denying free debate and expecting unquestioning loyalty, he will considerably weaken his own capability to succeed.

### An uncertain temper

It has been regularly observed that entrepreneurs are more likely to be prone to rapid mood changes than their colleagues in more conventional walks of life. It seems that a dominant ambition and a strong driving force to achieve a clearly visualized personal goal lead directly to impatience in the face of obstacles or inefficiencies. Some successful entrepreneurs have been described as "having a beguiling mixture of endless charm and a capacity for unbridled tyranny." They are more often optimistic and extroverted than pessimistic and introverted. To be successful they need sufficient self-control to present these positive qualities to those on whose judgments they rely. However, this does not always reflect the way in which they behave in private towards those who rely on them. For example, the cheerful, outgoing and caring individual known and loved by his customers, financiers, and fellow shareholders may be seen in a totally different light by his staff and suppliers. He may be intolerant, vindictive, and unreasonable without this being apparent outside the business. Inevitably, these personality traits leak out into the wider business community, where several examples can be found of highly successful entrepreneurs enjoying this "Jekyll and Hyde" reputation for their external image and internal behavior.

◆　◆　◆

Art Mathers, the founder and principal shareholder in a high-tech company, has a group of senior colleagues who are devoted to him and to the business. He has always shown a caring attitude towards them as individuals and their work within the company. However, as the business moves from a stage when survival is the most important issue to relative stability and success, his real temperament starts to emerge. It becomes clear that he is insecure in his ability to drive the business further forward and consequently looks for flattery and reassurance from his colleagues. Having received it, however, he becomes suspicious of the motives of the individual concerned and reacts harshly. Those who do not fall prey to this find themselves being dealt with rationally and irrationally in turn. Public applause is followed by private criticism, communicated indirectly through another colleague. The team becomes deeply conscious of, as one of them puts it, "walking on an organizational quicksand." Art's inconsistency in dealing with his colleagues, caused by his own insecurity, is at the root of the problem. Their own confidence in him rapidly declines despite the clear evidence of the continued success of the business. Art strives ever harder to gain the reassurance he needs but consistently fails. Ultimately, a confrontation occurs and the team deserts its erstwhile leader.

◆　◆　◆

It is a well-accepted management maxim that a consistently poor style is much to be preferred to one that is inconsistently good or bad. This applies even more strongly to the entrepreneur, since his relationships are built around much less conventional and hierarchical assumptions. An uncertain temper is usually a form of entrepreneurial self-indulgence, and the entrepreneur only gets away with it because of the compliance of colleagues and associates. High quality managers rarely tolerate this behavior in their bosses nor permit it in themselves. This sometimes explains why those managers supporting entrepreneurs are so often of such uninspiring quality.

## Unreliable leadership
There are many illustrations of leaders being unreliable, sometimes even misleading their subordinates to the extent that the team is wholly unprepared for the action in which they become engaged. The leader can cause confusion by rapid changes in strategy or tactics, or in

the distribution of roles to the members of his team. He can abandon his subordinates in the thick of the fray or fail to make crucial decisions when changes in direction are called for. Most of all, he can lose the confidence of those around him so that morale becomes irretrievably low.

Entrepreneurs are prone to any or all of these failings in precisely the same way as other business managers. The problem of identifying when and to what extent the failings occur, however, is much greater in the entrepreneurial environment since there is often little precedent to guide those involved and no rulebook to indicate normal procedures. By its very nature, entrepreneurialism is about innovation and risk-taking. In large companies "intrapreneurialism" is a surrogate for the process that happens in less structured environment. In a large company, however, there are frameworks within which the entrepreneurial process is encouraged and monitored. The individuals involved have certain expectations of the way in which plans and decisions are likely to be communicated and progress measured. The entrepreneur may, of course, already have precedents with earlier ventures on which his subordinates can call; he may have such an organized and distinctive style that any failings in leadership on his part are quickly identified and rectified. In many cases, however, this will not be possible and problems and potential failure could follow. Let us look at an example of this problem.

◆    ◆    ◆

Bill Daring is the promoter of a new venture involving the manufacture and sale of a new form of electric pump. Well versed in the background of the industry and the relevant technology, he brings together an able team of managers and raises the necessary funds to set the venture in motion. Initial indications are promising and the market take-off of the new product gives Bill and his colleagues cause for satisfaction. Then one Friday night, Bill departs unexpectedly on an overseas trip and leaves no forwarding address with his secretary. His colleagues are mystified and become alarmed when, on the following Monday, Bill's secretary circulates a letter from an English firm of lawyers claiming that the new product is in breach of a worldwide patent. The letter goes on to threaten the company with an injunction, demanding that they cease production forthwith. In Bill's absence the management team consults lawyers and manages to stave off the problem for three weeks, when a meeting is arranged with the English company and their lawyers. Desperate attempts to reach Bill fail, but calm is restored when he returns to the office a week later.

He confirms that the action taken by his team was absolutely correct, but also announces that he has to visit a major customer on the day of the crucial meeting with the English firm. Nothing will persuade him to change his plans and the management team is left to negotiate a settlement in his absence. They do their best, but can only achieve a royalty agreement which makes a considerable dent in the firm's profits. On his return, Bill is deeply dissatisfied with the arrangements and attempts to recover lost ground. The die has already been cast, however, and he has to reconcile himself to a much less prosperous future than he would otherwise have expected.

His colleagues are mystified and disappointed by his apparent lack of sensitivity to the importance of this issue. They suspect that he knew about the letter before leaving on his first trip and intentionally left them to resolve this particular crisis without his help and support. Whether true or not, the feelings deeply affect their confidence in Bill's judgment. He has failed them as a leader at a critical moment in the development of the company, and perhaps through less than honorable motives. It took a long time for the team to recover from this apparent lapse in his otherwise energetic and effective leadership.

◆   ◆   ◆

Those who set out to be successful entrepreneurs seldom, if ever, envisage that they may become victims of the Napoleon factor. They take on themselves, however, a significant responsibility to behave in a straightforward, consistent and effective way in their dealings with the people around them. They can be forgiven many shortcomings in terms of temper and attitude, but an insensitivity to wise counsel and an overweaning confidence in their own judgment can be harbingers of problems ahead.

## An impossible partner?
Much of our investigation so far has been concerned with the entrepreneur as the solo player—the individualist who pursues his own innovative goals with energy and enthusiasm. But sometimes entrepreneurs appear to operate in pairs or groups. Are these genuine team efforts?

Practical experience suggests that entrepreneurs are essentially dominant individuals and, therefore, any relationship between an entrepreneur and a "partner" is likely to be on a footing of the second individual being in some way subordinate to the first. Genuine equality may, of course, appear to be present to the casual observer—many successful trading empires have been founded by siblings, who show complementary mental attitudes or skills. One may be a more active risk-taker and one more conservative, while an outgoing personality may be matched by a more introverted one. They appear to take their decisions jointly and one will always consult the other.

In truth, harmonious partnerships are often not what they appear. Close relationships of this nature, particularly when innovation is involved, are seldom straightforward. The reason for the partners' coming together in the first place and the experiences they have shared both influence the way their mutual arrangement works. It may be driven by a sense of mutual benefits—the classic equation of two plus two making five, but whatever the age or relative status of the individuals, one or other always has the final word; successful entrepreneurial partnerships will always contain one individual whose judgment overrides the other when doubt arises (although which one of the two this is can, and sometimes does, change over time without any apparent loss of common momentum). Discovering which of the partners makes the decisions is vital if you are doing business with them.

If the entrepreneurial duo consists of brothers or sisters or father and son, similarity of temperament often proves a disadvantage rather than an advantage in terms of entrepreneurial drive. There can be no hard and fast rules, but entrepreneurs have a considerable need for someone close to them "off whom sparks can be struck." If the near relation is too much like the entrepreneur, the process is confirmatory of his judgments rather than challenging.

A good entrepreneurial partnership consists of a dominant individual and a subordinate with complementary but strongly held views. The element of respect for the other's judgment must feature large in such arrangements if they are to be permanent. Entrepreneurs are distrustful and dismissive of others' talents, hence the rarity of such partnerships. This is not to say that successful partnerships (husbands and wives are a good example) cannot do very well in finding and developing businesses. However, it is the degree of entrepreneurial challenge confronting the individuals that is the touchstone for success. For example, take a lease on a corner shop or establishing a successful country market is an admirable enterprise for a married couple, and many important decisions are doubtless involved. However, it is not comparable in scale of difficulty with another couple inventing, manufacturing and marketing a brand new product.

Few are privileged to hear the private conversations between the individuals involved in a genuinely creative and successful entrepreneurial partnership. Much will depend on the temperament, education and cultural background of the participants. However, it seems likely that planning, decision-making and trouble-shooting involve intense feelings and strong commitment vividly and energetically expressed. The creative genius of Gilbert and Sullivan resulted from an explosive personal relationship, and Messrs. Rolls and Royce did not enjoy a perennially harmonious working relationship.

The genuine entrepreneurial partner is a rare individual and undoubtedly needs exceptional qualities or strength of character, persistence and resilience. It is perhaps an accident of fate that brings such teams together and once formed they can be remarkably successful. The "love/hate" relationship seems a common factor but an essential one for them to work well.


## Follow my leader

Much more common than the entrepreneurial partner is the trusted lieutenant who is close to the entrepreneur but does not share in the final decision-making process. Many highly successful businessmen have acquired such individuals in the course of their business progress. They can have almost any background, qualifications, or set of personal attributes. The one common characteristic is that they support the entrepreneur (with total loyalty), aid and abet his activities, and perform whatever is asked of them, however trivial. The analogy used by some to describe such people is that of the devoted wife always available to do her husband's bidding. This seems a little unfair on most wives in these emancipated days and a more apt comparison might be with Jeeves or Figaro, but without the element of manipulation attributed to these two famous servants.

Such trusty lieutenants are often treated outrageously and inconsistently by the entrepreneur. Abuse, sarcasm, ill-will, and unreasonableness are commonplace in the case of some of the more extravagant and unpredictable entrepreneurs. The ability to tolerate and bounce back from such insensitive and unfair treatment is much admired by those less closely involved. It does raise the question, however, of why such individuals suffer these indignities rather than move elsewhere.

The answer appears to lie in the fascination which men of action and decision hold for many people. The charisma often associated with successful entrepreneurs is partly the self-confidence of the dominant individual and partly the command over people which money and power bring. This has a curious fascination for some people and can strongly influence the behavior of otherwise mature individuals.

Many people could not, and would not, tolerate the treatment meted out to these lieutenants. They, in turn, probably would not want to change their lot with anyone else and indeed they often assume positions of considerable power and influence themselves when the entrepreneur becomes more remote from his business operations. Perhaps they are following a more subtle course than most would credit them with.

## A team of heroes

Many of the most vaunted corporate entrepreneurs have built their personal reputations on closely organized teams of individuals. It is a characteristic of many high-technology industries that innovation is only possible as a team enterprise and the various technical and managerial skills needed to bring a major project to fruition are the province of highly motivated and expert individuals. The team can indeed be heroic in an entrepreneurial sense. However, every such team needs, and has always needed, someone who is its leader. As discussed earlier, entrepreneurs in a large corporate environment have a different role and behave in a different way from those operating outside that system. Their skills are more likely to emphasize planning, team-building and motivation than individual innovation and risk-taking. In economic terms, they are highly valuable to the country and in some sense are more influential in business development than the solo player. By their very rarity, the individuals involved often rise rapidly to positions of great prominence and corporate seniority. There is no doubt that a blending of the attitudes and skills of the individual entrepreneur and the organizational aptitude of his corporate colleague offers a remarkably effective team combination which, sadly, is seldom seen in practice.

Large corporations often seek to grow by acquiring smaller or entrepreneurial companies. This is frequently the case in high-technology industries in which technical breakthroughs are regularly made by small companies. The acquirer usually attempts to channel the vigorous enterprise of the owner of the small company to their mutual benefit.

It seldom works. The seller generally works out a contract "earn out" period before moving on, probably to set up another small business. The critical factor is usually the smothering effect of corporate bureaucracy, which ultimately deters the free thinking and decision-making of the individual who has previously been his own boss. Corporate entrepreneurialism thrives in a few large corporations because the people involved understand and know how to play the corporate game; self-made men seldom have the time or inclination to learn the rules.

# Living with a whirlwind

Sometimes, one comes across a director of a successful growing business who respects and is respected by the owner. He has done well in his role in the entrepreneur's team and managed to blend professionalism and enterprise. What is the secret?

The first rule is not to attempt to maintain either the entrepreneur's pace of work (which is usually exhausting to most people) or to keep abreast of his kaleidoscopic range of interests and activities. The director needs to have a strong sense of his personal role and identity and to act wholly consistently within it. For example, if the person concerned deals with finance, then he must understand and follow his own judgment with regard to the entrepreneur's financial affairs. He must have a consistent attitude towards risk-taking, financial probity, and stewardship and the disciplines needed in the organization and management of an effective company. These attitudes will undoubtedly bring him from time to time into conflict with the entrepreneur. He may be the butt of the latter's sense of frustration or have his loyalty questioned, but being true to his own beliefs and standards will ultimately be the most powerful contribution he can make to the team effort. Undoubtedly, the director concerned must have a thick skin, not be too easily put off by apparently eccentric behavior, or lose confidence if his boss fails to observe the niceties of a conventional organization. Successful entrepreneurs ultimately respect strong-minded colleagues and do not expect their subordinates either to ape their own behavior or be yes men. The experience of working with a successful entrepreneur is a great test of character and will for many younger managers; there is an almost irresistible temptation to become a carbon copy of the boss. It is amusing and somewhat sad to visit an entrepreneurially led company to find directors and managers alike using language and gestures which directly echo those of the dominant entrepreneur involved.

Most of all, people working for entrepreneurs need a very clear view of what they can contribute to the overall success of the enterprise. When ventures are first being set up, roles may be very confused, but the end objective is very clear; the team spirit that encourages everyone to get involved in any menial task is both exhilarating and effective. As entrepreneurial enterprises grow, roles become clearer, but the end objective becomes less apparent. This is a result of the impatience which entrepreneurs sometimes have with conventional management structures and decision-making mechanisms. Thus the finance director quoted earlier may be asked to play a variety of roles depending on the immediate priorities of his boss. At one moment the operation of the petty cash control system may be under close scrutiny and at the next he may have to explain the company's long-term funding strategy in layman's terms. It is this very variety which many find the most appealing thing about working so close to the whirlwind. A calm head and a good sense of humor are also invaluable personal characteristics for those who want to make a long-term career in such people's company.

## 24 hours a day

Many successful entrepreneurs take pride in their unwillingness to take holidays. "One day off in the last five years" was the boast of the owner of a successful hotel chain; an equally common expression is that "my work is my hobby"—which to the uninitiated is either mysterious or enviable or both.

Undoubtedly, long hours and reluctantly taken vacations are a hallmark of the dedicated entrepreneur. Neglected wives and girlfriends may well use the disparaging term "workaholic" to describe this demonic pursuit of business. The interesting question is, what is the "work" involved and how does it compare with that done by people in more conventional jobs?

In an earlier chapter it was argued that the entrepreneur continually creates a very clear vision of the world as he wishes to see and influence it. The vision may be of every teenager wearing his brand of socks or of his commanding the most prestigious and profitable firm of advertising agents. If he is a dealer his vision is that of the successful transaction and the profits which will flow from it.

The entrepreneur's "work" is therefore the process of bringing his vision to a reality. This process is rather like the Chinese juggler spinning a series of plates on bamboo canes. As a new plate is set spinning the juggler must return to those started earlier to keep up their momentum. The action becomes frenetic as more plates are spun, and the danger of one or more falling from its pole increases. Like the Chinese juggler, the entrepreneur sees the end state of all the plates spinning as his personal vision. His energies are spent on keeping all the components working towards that common end.

The equivalent to the spinning plates in the entrepreneur's life is the attitude and decisions of those on whom he relies to carry out his plans. Research has shown that influential individuals spend between 70 and 80 percent of their working days in conversation with others either face to face or on the telephone. These conversations are as much to do with information gathering and persuading as with decision-making. The entrepreneur is clearly at the center of the decision-making process, but the process itself is often very swift. The ability to see the required decision in the context of the long-term plan is frequently exclusively that of the entrepreneur rather than of those around him. This gives him a considerable advantage in the speed and clarity of his decision-making.

The entrepreneur's working day typically includes some strenuous physical activity even if it is restricted to a gallop around the shop floor or a chase across the tarmac to the private jet. Spare moments are spent in reading what is often a wide and ill-assorted selection of newspapers and magazines (entrepreneurs are seldom bookish) and some time in private and quiet reflection. Habits of writing or dictating letters or memoranda vary considerably, but as a general rule entrepreneurs prefer to have three or four phones in the office, with a portable phone, and leave it to others to prepare anything beyond a short and crisp directive.

The characteristic energy charge such individuals bring to their daily work is often accompanies by a low boredom threshold and a desire for variety of company and topics. This can be deceptive since the art of winning support and influencing people often demands care and patience and single-minded concentration.

This mixture of activity involves little that is routine and much that contributes to the self-generated excitement of the risk-taker. The lack of structure in itself clearly offers a sense of satisfaction to the entrepreneur. More importantly, he almost certainly feels that nothing outside his sphere of work has any comparable significance. The self-centered "universe," which is so extraordinarily real to the entrepreneur, often represents a curiously unbalanced view of life as seen by the independent observer. Work becomes a passion and pervades the individual's life, often to the exclusion of all other significant interests. Even though the entrepreneur may become known as a leading collector or philanthropist, it often seems that this is no more than a diversion from what really matters—business!

Many successful men appear to find it very difficult to enjoy the wealth they have worked so hard to earn. Brief excursions on the luxury yacht or to the hideaway on an exotic island are interrupted by frequent, and perhaps solicited, business calls. The grim determination of a relaxing entrepreneur intent on enjoying himself, come what may, is alarming and dispiriting to behold. The excitement in his life, born of his business interests, acts as a powerful motivator and potential narcotic. He is unhappy and impatient whenever the stimulus is removed.

◆　◆　◆

A real life example is the case of a real estate tycoon whose career started in his teens when he worked as a negotiator for an estate agent. Spotting the potential of an undervalued property, he persuaded a wealthy car dealer to buy the derelict building for which he then obtained planning consent. This original deal led to more joint venture initiatives and in due course to his forming his own company. He traveled the length and breadth of the country in search of sites with potential, working evenings and weekends, holidays, and even on Christmas Day. Soon his business had grown to the size at which he could afford to recruit professional staff, who had the skill and experience to relieve him of much of the burden of site visits, negotiations with vendors, and money-raising forays to the bank. Rather than reduce his workload or change his style of operation, he allowed his personal workload actually to increase. His pattern of supervising every detail meant that, as the company grew, he had even more to oversee. An obvious consequence of this process was that he suffered from a build-up of mental and physical exhaustion, which resulted in a breakdown from which he never fully recovered. He agreed that the cause had been totally illogical; he went on to admit that his lifestyle, as the company had grown, had become less agreeable than when he was only accountable to himself.

The commitment to his private world was nonetheless so total that he was willing to put his health at risk. Like many successful men, he suffered from the problems of "boundary vision" in the form of an inability to see his own enterprise in the context of the wider world.

◆　◆　◆

It has been argued that a period of such total commitment is essential to the process of building a successful business. In time, the individual emerges from this stage with a more balanced view of his own role and that of the organization he has built.

## Money and power

All the available research shows that, in the early stages of entrepreneurial development at least, it is the drive to become rich that is the prime motivator. A recent survey of entrepreneurs demonstrated that they are drawn from a wide variety of cultural and domestic backgrounds. It would certainly be untrue to assume that the entrepreneur always springs from a background of deprivation and is motivated to catch up with his more affluent colleagues. Many of the most successful have either inherited wealth or married into money and have used this as the lever for the development of a greater fortune. Whether the pursuit of wealth is seen as an end in itself or simply as the means of accumulating more is something of a puzzle. If the premise that the entrepreneur is particularly conscious of the insecurity of his position is correct, then the urge to accumulate wealth could be explained in terms of that factor alone. The need for financial security is satisfied at a relatively modest level for most people, but the entrepreneur drives onward with an apparently insatiable desire to accumulate yet more.

The paradox of piling increasing riches on wealth already gained is that it appears to have less and less influence over the entrepreneur's behavior. Indeed, there comes a point at which the financial factor in any business equation is more meaningful to the entrepreneur in relative than in absolute terms. Thus the international trading magnate with a personal wealth of, say, $500 million is less interested in the actual cost of mounting a predatory bid on another company than in the rate of profit or capital growth he can anticipate on the deal relative to his other activities. The financial motive then becomes more refined and academic in its impact on the entrepreneur's behavior, although the judgments he makes may remain fairly subjective and crude.

The phases of the development of this financial motivation can be characterized as follows:

- Conspicuous spending.
- Fortune building.
- Aestheticism.

### Conspicuous spending

The nascent entrepreneur is probably motivated as much by the things money can buy as by the leverage it gives over the growth of the business. The degree of conspicuousness will, of course, depend very much on the temperament of the individual. It may be overt and flashy or subtle and understated. It is almost always there, however, as a tangible demonstration that the individual has "made it." Houses, cars, luxury holidays, furniture, pictures, or other *objets d'art* are usually the sign of the "new" rich. Simply to have them is not sufficient, of course: they must be advertised and recognized by the entrepreneur's peer group. This rather crude exhibitionism is found neither universally nor consistently. However, it is sufficiently common to be regarded as a distinctive feature which, in some cases, remains unchanged throughout the entrepreneur's career. For most, the lifestyle satisfactions arising from newly acquired wealth start to fall into a pattern that needs no further priming by new spending and the motivating force changes. The entrepreneur then finds himself in the fortune-building phase.

## Fortune building

In this phase, the entrepreneur becomes deeply aware of his own financial progress and achievement and is often very cautious and careful of its management. For many, this phase becomes a lifelong preoccupation; there are thousands of family businesses in which the founder has successfully handed down a substantial fortune as a consequence of prudent financial management.

The financial motive remains as strong as ever, but the result of his activities are handled with discretion and perhaps even secrecy. Entrepreneurs do not have to be reclusive to disguise the range and nature of their interests from the casual observer. For example, local gossip in a market town may attribute involvement in many ventures to a successful businessman who, in fact, has no part in them at all. The veil which the entrepreneur can draw over his affairs is usually penetrated by few other than his accountant and the tax man. This frequently works to his advantage in enabling him to create a reputation of success on the one hand and to disguise his failures on the other.

For most, the fortune-building stage starts when, perhaps, the individual's personal wealth exceeds $1 million and may continue to levels well in excess of $100 million. Above these figures, however, the third phase—aestheticism—starts to appear.

## Aestheticism

With a substantial and secure fortune behind him, the active entrepreneur starts to attach a more symbolic meaning to wealth and the motivation of money than in the previous phases. Under all reasonable analysis, the fortune at his disposal, unless it is precariously invested in one particular enterprise, gives him and his kin whatever security and lifestyle they might reasonably need for the foreseeable future. The basic appetites for these have long since been satisfied. The drive for further wealth accumulation continues, and even accelerates, because it is the process of entrepreneurship and the symbolic measurement of its success in financial terms that is more appealing than the actual money itself. Although not truly aesthetic, the financial sophistication and manipulative skills of the heavyweight operator often have a clinical objectivity which comes close to this epithet. This style of thinking is perhaps most evident in those who act as "traders" under our earlier classification of entrepreneurial types. Buying and selling companies, forming new and aggressive liaisons, breaking up enterprises and dealing with governments are all grist to the mill at this most visible and high level of entrepreneurialism. The transactions involved are often highly complex and structured in very sophisticated ways. The financial ingredients are dominant and social; cultural and personal interests are frequently the least significant. The creation, planning and execution of these types of deals often have a stark simplicity with the financial consequence as their only "reality." At this stage the entrepreneur becomes a game-player, with the financial stakes being no more real than the plastic chips at the roulette table. The drive to accumulate more is no less remorseless, but the emphasis is on winning rather than on the number of chips themselves.

### The urge for power

Money can clearly bring power to the entrepreneur in terms of commanding the world about him. At its simplest level, the successful man's ability to live more luxuriously, drive faster cars, and command more attention from tailors and head waiters is proof positive to him that he stands above the common man. This simple aspect of entrepreneurial power becomes more complex as the individual's influence itself grows. The strongest element is probably his power over people. Successful entrepreneurs often claim disinterest in this aspect and a benign approach to those who work for them. Both assertions should be treated with some suspicion.

The *bonhomie* of the workplace between the owner of the business and his shop-floor employee often disguises the mutual recognition of the boss's power to decide his subordinate's future in the business. There is nothing inherently wrong with this relationship, but its presentation as something different from what it actually is can cause some disquiet. If the entrepreneur behaves consistently and fairly to his colleagues, he will earn their confidence and respect. The very nature of the entrepreneurial activity, however, often demands a ruthlessness in dealing with people, which many find distasteful. From the viewpoint of the entrepreneur, people are frequently no more than one element in a complex equation. Further, they are an element without significant individuality and their prime function is to facilitate the operation of the other parts.

Some entrepreneurs seem to delight in demonstrating their power over their subordinates through, for example, embarrassing or belittling them in front of their colleagues or demanding menial services of senior individuals. An entrepreneur rampant at a board meeting can be a frightening sight. His power over the destiny of his colleagues is sometimes so great that what elsewhere would be considered outrageous behavior is accepted as being tolerable. Zoologists might suggest that the pack leader is doing no more than demonstrating his dominance over those who might challenge his position. This may be so, but the curious fact is that the remarkable powers of persuasion and not infrequent mood changes of entrepreneurs often enable them to retain the loyalty of their colleagues, which might otherwise be lost through these demonstrations of authority.

The second power arena is that which the entrepreneur has over organizations external to the enterprise itself. Typically, the successful entrepreneur finds that he can directly or indirectly influence the destiny of, for example, a supplier organization. Suppliers and customers often prosper together, but the supplier's problem is frequently that of over-dependence on his principal customer. This can put considerable potential for powerful manipulation in the hands of the customer. Equally, the third party could be a trade association, a community, or a local political party. Whatever the dimensions of the external body, the successful entrepreneur can often exercise a powerful influence over their judgments and decisions. This power of patronage is a strong motivating force which the entrepreneur can put to good (or bad) use.

The motive for exercising power and influence in such situations can sometimes be traced back to the entrepreneur's underlying wish to be recognized. Despite being critical of established institutions, entrepreneurs are often more than ready to accept their accolades. Thus, chairmanships of charitable bodies, boards of school governors or health authorities, honorary degrees, or other titles prove remarkably agreeable to those who have spent their earlier careers castigating the establishment. The reality of power and the extent of over recognition of personal achievement become blurred in these more mature stages of the entrepreneurs' careers. Many businessmen have much more real power over people when operating in private than when holding some eminent public office.

Lastly, there is the power the entrepreneur wields over the development of products, markets, and consumer behavior. To be able to say that you have changed the course of economic development through the introduction of a new material or product is to recognize a special form of power. The urge to innovate links directly to the satisfactions to be gained from this source. The mixture of these three essential ingredients will vary from one mdividual to another. In the last analysis, however, a combination of money and power proves irresistible.

## Family man

As dominant individualists it is hardly surprising that many entrepreneurs prove difficult marriage partners. There are examples of highly successful husband-and-wife entrepreneurial partnerships, which suggest that a like-minded attitude towards the excitement of wealth creation has a strong mutual attraction. In public, such marital partnerships often present a powerful and persuasive image. As argued earlier, however, all entrepreneurial duos contain one individual whose judgment and influence is significantly more powerful than the other. The same is invariably true of the more private lives of married couples, whether or not they work together in business. In many areas of business, particularly those involving services, a husband-and-wife team is an attractive promotional proposition. In reality, the one who is the "junior" partner is likely to have a fairly stressful existence unless well tuned to the particular role he or she is asked to play.

That role can range from keeping a high public profile to extreme domestic privacy. In the former case, the male entrepreneur often seems to want to share his success in public with his wife; in the latter, he clearly separates his more visible business activities from his private life. Thus, his wife may become as well known as the husband himself.

## Private lives

In private, entrepreneurs' wives (or husbands) have to deal with individuals whose temperament and approach to life can make them extremely difficult to live with. An entrepreneur's wife confided that her husband was:

- More interested in anything connected with the business than with his wife and family.
- Impatient and short-tempered, sometimes treating the domestic situation as a simple extension of the challenges of business.
- Unable to relax and enjoy fully leisure activities with the family.
- Of variable moods, depending on the pressures of his business life.

This may seem rather an extreme case, but the high emotional charge associated with the wealth-creation process must often leave the entrepreneur drained of energy and enthusiasm for more mundane interests. Experience suggests that such people recognize at an early stage in their careers that they will benefit from marriage. A supportive wife can be a crucial factor in making difficult decisions, despite the fact that the responsibility of the family man is much greater than that of the bachelor. Entrepreneurs, therefore, tend to marry at a relatively early age and at the beginning of their careers. In consequence,they encounter the problems of developing their own personality and lifestyle at a pace and in a direction which may not be matched by that of their partners. Neither may originally envisage the nature of the demands to be made on each other. The day-to-day pressures on the relationship, particularly when the personal and financial risks involved are extreme, can be enormous. It is these pressures most evident in private life that can cause the spectacular marriage break-ups often associated with the successful businessman.

An argument can be made for the case that entrepreneurs are essentially loners and that any form of permanent personal relationship runs counter to their nature. This loneliness itself stems from a feeling of being at odds with the world and the constant desire to demonstrate individual success. While there is some truth to be found in this analysis, it denies the obvious effects of the passage of time. Older and more experienced people inevitably become more circumspect in their behavior and often see changing values in their personal relationships. Thus, the importance of the family and, in particular, the role of the entrepreneur's children, gain more importance as his own career moves through middle age. The image of the contented self-made man, benevolent to those around him, handing on his business to a grateful younger generation, is as far-fetched as that of the miserly recluse hoarding his missions. As a general rule, however, it seems that entrepreneurs become relatively easier to live with as they get older and experience tempers the fiery impatience of youth.

## Keeping it in the family

The question of nepotism is one that deeply affects many who have succeeded in building a successful enterprise. It seems to them almost an affront that a younger generation should have any reservation about taking on the stewardship of the family future. For the entrepreneur, it is the ultimate disappointment if that generation simply wishes to enjoy the financial spoils without accepting some mantle of continued business involvement.

When asked the question, "What is all this exhausting expenditure of time and effort for?" the reply will frequently be, "For the benefit of my family." The truth is that the family is seldom consulted and the entrepreneur makes assumptions about its interests which frequently prove unfounded.

Public markets for shares have grown enormously in recent years and flotation is no longer a privilege accorded only to large and established companies. Business founders increasingly see the benefit of having their equity interest reflected in marketable securities. In theory, at least, they can easily sell their shares, if they so wish, at a price that considerably exceeds that available to a private company. There are, of course, some disadvantages. A public company is very much in the public eye and the principal shareholder may find himself more accountable to the marketplace and to the commentary (whether complimentary or critical) of financial analysts. A quoted company is also more vulnerable to unwelcome and predatory takeovers. Nonetheless, many family enterprises that would, in earlier times, have remained just that lose their unique entrepreneurial identity within a single generation.

A dynastic approach to business is much less common now than it was 50 or 100 years ago. Many entrepreneurs are selling their businesses in early middle age and perhaps going on to found another fortune, having provided for their family from the first. The reason is that there is no longer an automatic succession of children to family businesses. This is partly because nowadays children are both better educated and have a wider range of personal choice. It is also because the social assumptions surrounding businesses have themselves changed and a recognition of the need for professional management is more widespread. Thus the old adage "from rags to riches and back again in three generations" is seen by many as very true. The entrepreneurial wizardry of one generation is seldom if ever perpetuated by the next. Even entrepreneurs themselves, albeit reluctantly, now recognize that the handing on of power is seldom either desirable or practical.

The reality is that the fortune has to be handed down to a new generation of owners who are likely to be supported by professional managers and advisers rather than being directly involved in the wealth-creation process themselves. The entrepreneur most recognizes the role of his successors quite some time before he is in a position to hand over the reins. This can be a painful and difficult process for him and his immediate family. It can involve strong feelings of guilt on each side and, as a result, quite irrational and unreasonable behavior. An entrepreneur's son might, for example, "drop out" and take to a dissolute life rather than face up to the reality of his unwillingness to become involved in the family business. The father might fail to understand the underlying cause of his son's behavior and, try as he might, have little influence over it until this root cause is recognized.

These problems are often further complicated by feelings of inadequacy in a particularly successful and powerful parent. The psychology is complex and needs a fair degree of thought and self-analysis on the part of the entrepreneur. This is often not the strong point of the individual concerned and a crisis occurs through lack of sensible forethought. The symptoms are often plain to see from the standpoint of the outsider, but are swept to one side by the busy and successful business builder.

## Summary

The entrepreneur can easily become a prima donna in both his relationships with those who work for him and those who share his private life. Some of the characteristics of a prima donna are essential to the success of the individual; they help him to be single-minded and energetic in his approach to the challenges of his career. On the other hand, they can make him an uncomfortable and difficult colleague who would be unbearable company if it weren't for the special talents and abilities that he brings to his primary role as innovator and business developer. He is often an unsuccessful family man, married more closely to his business than his wife. Although middle age often brings a change in values, by then it is often too late.

*Chapter 7*

# Summing up

Our investigation has led us through most aspects of the life and behavior of the entrepreneur. Much of the evidence is conflicting and the available research, such as it is, incomplete; many of the conclusions that can be drawn are inevitably controversial while others are no more than statements of the self-evident. In any event, there must be a ready and absolute recognition that we are not dealing with a comfortably classifiable species with definable characteristics and behavior. Entrepreneurs have always sprung, and will doubtless continue to spring, from a variety of backgrounds and personal circumstances, and attempts at generalization would be dangerous. And yet powerful evidence supports the notion that certain elements of attitudes, motives, and behavior occur so frequently that a pattern is discernible.

This pattern, the "character set" as one may call it, has been the principal focus of this book and the common thread of argument running through it. Many entrepreneurs surround themselves with an aura of mystique which sometimes verges on a personal mythology. As they mature and prosper they have an ever-increasing interest in its perpetuation and enhancement—it is all part of the projection of an image of themselves they wish to impose on the world. It satisfies not only their needs, but also those of others who lack the curiosity or opportunity to inquire more deeply.

This image of the entrepreneur offers us folk heroes in an age dominated by the faceless corporatism, but is it accurate? Does it give a true description of the man as he really is rather than as he would like us to see him? "No man is a hero to his valet" is an old but wise adage. In his nakedness, does the entrepreneur live up to our expectations, or is there a dark side to his nature and his behavior?

The simple answer to these questions is that entrepreneurs are exceptional individuals in whom certain common character traits are so highly accentuated (or, if you like, distorted) that they behave quite abnormally compared to the rest of us. Their economic influence is generally beneficial: they break the rules, innovate, take risks, and create wealth (not least for themselves); their personal behavior is often partial, unpredictable, unfair, and destructive; their enterprise brings benefits to society at large, but their personal behavior is likely to have a disturbing effect on their colleagues and associates. They are by turns benefactors and rebels—an admirable group of men and women with much to teach us about enterprise and much to warn us of in terms of exaggerated personal style.

## Alike or different?

By concentrating on the character set of entrepreneurs, we draw together those aspects entrepreneurs are likely to have in common. To this extent they can be said to be "alike." Equally, the great diversity of activities and businesses in which they engage should be acknowledged. There seems to be no aspect of industry, commerce, or services which does not throw up potential opportunities for the budding entrepreneur. Whether innovative in the true sense of creating a new product or service or simply exploiting the application of an old one, the scope seems boundless. Nor is it limited by age, means or educational background. The "incubator" theory suggests that some individuals need the right environment in which to develop their nascent talents. Conversely, many entrepreneurs (and especially those with a strong trading instinct) start their careers well before they have entered the structured world of business.

Both men and women show talent for entrepreneurialism, although the great majority of entrepreneurs to date are male—a reflection perhaps on the reality of equal opportunity rather than on the theory. Failure rates are high and many venture capitalists would give their eyeteeth for the skill of invariably spotting the winners.

In all these respects, entrepreneurs are as different from one another as they are from the rest of us. They have, however, much more in common than they may readily admit to; the pattern constantly recurs. It is in recognizing this and building upon it that the future of a more positive approach to entrepreneurialism can be developed.

## Developing entrepreneurial capacity

The essence of a more positive approach must be to reduce the "accidental" way in which incipient talents are brought to mature realization. In a society geared to rewarding conformity, this is no easy task. In essence, it requires:

- An early recognition of relevant talents.
- A conscious commitment to creating the most propitious environment for their development.
- A changed attitude towards failure.

In the Introduction we listed a number of "tendencies," which single out the entrepreneur from his fellow men. These are likely to show themselves in school, at college, or in the early stages of employment. With some honorable exceptions, the institutions involved act generally to suppress or inhibit them, since they are seen to be either disruptive or anti-cultural. The frustration this causes may, of course, serve to make such individuals more purposeful and act as a coarse "filter" in selecting the more robust from their weaker brethren. It is more likely that it defers the development of nascent talent and restricts its opportunity. The argument can be made, therefore, that where the pattern is recognized, the obligation of the institution should be to encourage and foster it (with all the attendant risks) rather than to suppress it.

Employers bound by conventional notions of authority and hierarchy normally find it difficult to provide the "incubator" conditions in which potential entrepreneurs can spread their wings Strangely enough, small, entrepreneurially led businesses are usually the worst breeding grounds and large organizations the best. Institutionally organized firms struggle with concepts of "intrapreneurship," but very rarely prove capable of delivering the freedom and support the individual needs. Management buyouts that produce "born-again capitalists" frequently reveal an entrepreneurial capacity wholly unrecognized under more conventional management regimes. Developing an internal enterprise culture within a large firm is no easy matter. However, it *can* be done if the rewards of success (capital growth, esteem, freedom of action, and so on) are recognized as realistically as the penalties of failure.

Failure is often seen as the "tempering" by which the metal of the entrepreneur's abilities are proved. Attitudes to failure vary widely, both between those promoting ventures and those backing them. However, a more rational approach to entrepreneurialism will only be developed if:

- A more rigorous approach is adopted to recognizing failure.
- It is seen as part of a learning process.

A more rigorous approach means dealing crisply and surgically with a venture when it fails rather than delaying, fudging, and temporizing when the inevitable is clearly unavoidable. Both entrepreneurs and backers are frequently equally guilty in this regard. Failure as part of the learning process suggests that if the basic talents are there the beneficial lessons should be emphasized rather than the loss of credibility or venture investment.

Each of these factors offers an opportunity to increase the "hit rate" in terms of both the number of potential entrepreneurs identified and encouraged, and the business success achieved.

## Golden rules for the entrepreneur

But what of the entrepreneur himself? His chosen career is lonely, fraught with risk, and beset with difficulty and potential failure. He is scorned if he fails and probably disliked if he succeeds. Success itself may bring no more than a renewed urge to pursue a personal regime that is exhausting physically, mentally and emotionally. What golden rules should he follow?

*Rule 1.* Know yourself
The incidence of self-delusion among entrepreneurs is astonishingly high. In small doses it is not only harmless, but also positively beneficial; in large doses it usually leads to failure. If the entrepreneur finds understanding himself a tough process, he should turn to a reliable and frank confidant.

*Rule 2.* Be thorough
He should take note of the saying "For the want of a nail the shoe was lost, for the want of a shoe the horse was lost, for the want of a horse the battle was lost." Many brilliantly conceived entrepreneurial schemes fail through some minor oversight. There is no one to blame but the entrepreneur himself.

*Rule 3.* Be consistent
However variable his temperament and attitude to people, he must try hard to act consistently. Nothing discomforts the people around the entrepreneur more than not knowing from one moment to the next

how he will react to a given situation. Keeping them on their toes is one thing; destroying their ability to act effectively is another.

*Rule 4.* Cut your losses
It does not matter a bit whether or not the entrepreneur is a good (or bad) loser. What matters is that he should recognize and deal with an inevitable failure before others take that initiative for him. This is not to suggest that the convinced entrepreneur should not persist in his attempts to prove that success can be achieved long after others have fallen by the wayside. It simply means that when he recognizes the inevitable he should act swiftly.

*Rule 5.* Look for crossroads
There are crossroads at various points in an entrepreneur's career, and these are frequently overlooked at the expense of later frustration or discontent. One occurs when the first fortune is made, giving him enough money to cater to all his material needs. The second may be when choices between domestic, "quality of life" activities and business options have to be made. The choice of developing a different, less involved management approach (or not) may be another. If crossroads are properly recognized and the choices analyzed, the entrepreneur will at least be more in charge of his destiny than might otherwise be the case.

*Rule 6.* Be prepared for change
This is the most difficult, but probably the most crucial, of the golden rules. Progress relies on change—change in attitudes and skills, change resulting from learning from experience, change induced by the influence of friends and associates and by the example of successful peers. Success achieved too easily (or too early) can suggest a degree of infallibility that is, in truth, illusory. Entrepreneurialism is not, and can never be, about formulas or standard methods. It relies on the inspiration to take advantage of circumstances undergoing change. This requires the entrepreneur himself to change, to sharpen his skills, and to build on his business achievements by constantly receiving, and if needed, reviewing his approach.

## The naked entrepreneur
We find, stripped of the self-seeking promotion and the adulation of the gossip columns a workaholic dedicated to the pursuit of wealth and power. Complex in his makeup, often careless of personal relation-

ships, he has a view of the world which is very different from the rest of us. He is in charge of his destiny, embraces extraordinary risks, but in many respects acts with caution and circumspection. His enthusiasm for his career gains momentum rather than loses it as material success is achieved. Winning the competitive "game" is more important than the financial stakes, which become mere counters on the board. Megalomania waits in the wings while the world both envies and dislikes continued success. Seldom lovable but always exciting to work with, and for, entrepreneurs are mainsprings in an enterprise culture. Long may they remain so.

# Bibliography

**Books**

Meredith, Nelson and Neck, *Practice of Entrepreneurship* (International Labor Office, 1985).

Drucker, Peter, *Innovation and Entrepreneurship* (Heinemann, 1985).

Chudley, John, *Letraset—A Lesson in Growth* (Business Books Ltd, 1974).

Additionally, there are numerous popular biographies and autobiographies of individual entrepreneurs.

**Research paper**

Birley, Sue and Watson, Liz, *The British Entrepreneur 1988* (Cranfield School of Management and Arthur Young).

**Articles**

Stevenson, Howard H. and Gumpert, David E., "The Heart of Entrepreneurship" (*Harvard Business Review*, March-April 1985).

Burch, John G., "Profiling the Entrepreneur" (*Business Horizons*, September-October 1986).

Cromie, Dr. Stanley, "Motivations of Aspiring Male and Female Entrepreneurs (*Journal of Occupational Behavior*, Vol. 251-261, 1978).

Clutterbuck, David and Devine, Marion, "Why Start Ups Start" (*Management Today*, July 1985).

Unattributed, "What Makes an Entrepreneur?" (*Director*, July 1986).

Cranston, H.S. and Glamholtz, Eric G., "The Role of Management Development in Making the Transition from an Entrepreneurship to a Professionally Managed Organization: (*Journal of Management Development*, Vol. 5, No. 1, 1986).

Chell, Elizabeth, "The Entrepreneurial Personality: A Few Ghosts Laid to Rest?" (*International Small Business Journal*, Spring 1985).

Reich, Robert B., "Entrepreneurship Reconsidered: The Team as Hero" (*Harvard Business Review*, May-June 1987).

Longenecker, Justin G., McKinney, Joseph A., and Moore, Carlos W., "Egoism and Independence: Entrepreneurial Ethics" (*Organization Dynamics*, October 1988).

Branson, Richard, "Risk Taking" (*Journal of General Management*, Vol II, No. 2, Winter 1985).

Kets de Vries, Manfred F.R., "The Dark Side of Entrepreneurship" (*Harvard Business Review*, November-December 1985).

Kaplan, Roger, "Entrepreneurship Reconsidered: The Anti-management Bias" (*Harvard Business Review*, May-June 1987).

Boyd, David P. and Gumpert, David E., "Coping With Entrepreneurial Stress" (*Harvard Business Review*, March-April 1983).

Solomon, George T. and Fernald, Lloyd W., "Value Profiles of Male and Female Entrepreneurs" (*International Small Business Journal*, April-June 1988).

Gumpert, David E. and Boyd, David P., "The Loneliness of the Small-Business Owner" (*Harvard Business Review*, November-December 1984).

Routamaa, Vesa and Vasalainen, Jukka, "Types of Entrepreneur and Strategic Level Goal Setting" (*International Small Business Journal*, Spring 1987).

Weinshall, Theodore D. and Vickery, Lister, "Entrepreneurs: A Balanced View of their Role in Innovation and Growth" (*European Management Journal*, Winter 1987).

Cooper, Arnold C. and Dunkelberg, William C., "Entrepreneurship and Paths to Business" (*Strategic Management Journal*, January-Frebruary 1986).

Smith, Ken G., Gannon, Martin J., Grimm, Curtis, and Mitchell, Terence R., "Decision-Making Behavior in Smaller Entrepreneurial and Larger Professionally Managed Firms" (*Journal of Business Venturing*, Summer 1988).

Covin, Jeffrey G. and Slevin, Dennis P., "The Influence of Organization Structure on the Utility of an Entrepreneurial Top Management Style" (*Journal of Management Studies*, May 1988).

Stevenson, Howard H. and Jarrillo-Mossi, Carlos, "Preserving Entrepreneurship as Companies Grow" (*The Journal of Business Strategy*, Summer 1986).

Matthews, Glenn H., "Run Your Business or Build an Organization" (*Harvard Business Review*, March-April 1984).

Firnstahl, Timothy W., "Letting Go" (*Harvard Business Review*, September-October 1986).

Slatter, Stuart, Ransley, Roy and Woods, Elizabeth, "USM Chief Executives: Do They Fit the Entrepreneurial Stereotype?" (*International Small Business Journal*, Vol. 6, No. 3).

# Index

References in *italics* indicate figures or tables.

achievement, desire for, 12
    *see also* competitiveness
administrative culture, entrepeneurial compared, 65-71, *66-67*
aestheticism, 98-99
African consulting assignment, trust example, 54
air travel, rule-breaking example, 54
applause-seeking, 51
Arthur Young/Cranfield study, 32
automotive industry launches, 43

Baird, John Logie, 21
behavior reliability see consistency
boat building, loyalty example, 85
book copying, salesmanship example, 24
boredom thresholds, 95
borrowing capacity, 47
"boundary vision," 96
Branson, Richard, 45, 59
Burch, John G., 11, 13, *14*, 111
bureaucratic culture, entrepreneurial compared 65-71, *66-67*
*Business Horizons*, 11
buying behavior, understanding, 24-25

candy selling, individualist example, 56
change and progress, golden rule, 109
Channel Tunnel, 21
"character set," 105-106
"charisma," 76, 91

children, 101-104
"climate" changes, 21
Clore, Sir Charles, 79
clothing factories, management example, 69-70
communication skills, 25, 61, 76
comparative risk-reward ratios, 45
competitiveness, 29-31, 53-54
concert parties, 34-36
conditioning theories, 11-13, 50-51
conduct, 36-37
    see also ethics; rule-breaking
"confidants," 55
"confidential briefings," 76
consistency of behavior, 87-89, 108-109
    and business growth, 61
    uncertain temper, 86-87
conspicuous spending, 97-98
"control, locus of," 50
conventional, intolerance of, 49-50
corporate entrepreneurialism, 92
Cranfield School of Management/Arthur Young survey, 32
crossroads, in career, 71, 109
cumulative risk profile, 46
customer behavior, 39-41

"Dark Side of Entrepreneurship, The," 29-30, 49, 112
Davies, Dai, 20
dealers, 27-28
decision points, career, 71, 109
decision-making, 94-95
despotism, 53
detail, attention to, 70-71
development of entrepreneurial capacity, 106-109
directors, 93
dismissal, of colleagues, 77
distrust, 53-56
"downside" risk assessment, 43-48
Drucker, Peter, 17, 111

electric pump venture, unreliability example, 88-89
electronic manservant, customer knowledge example, 40
"entrepreneur" definition, 9-10, 109
entrepreneur-managers, 81-82
entrepreneurial culture, administrative compared, 65-71, 66-67
entrepreneurial "echo," 59
entrepreneurial tendencies, 13-15, 14
ethics, management, 79-80
    see also rule-breaking

Europe, attitude toward failure, 31
excellence orientation, 12

failure, 31-33, 63, 107-108, 109
    early symptoms, 84-88
family relationships, 101-104
    children 102-104
    spouse, 101-102
financial motives, 26, 55, 96-101
"fixated" attitude, 20-22
fortune-building, 98

gamblers, 27, 43
grocery packaging, "hunch" example, 63
Gumpert, David, 65, 112

hard work, capacity for, 12, 13, 94-96
*Harvard Business Review*, 29-30, 65, 112
"Heart of Entrepreneurship, The," 65, 111
high-tech company, inconsistency example, 87
hula hoop, innovation example, 19
"hunch" factor, 62-63
husbands, 101-102

imagination, 19, 41
importance, need for feeling of, 37-38
inborn characteristics, 11-13, 50, 105-106
incongruities, search for, 18-21
inconsistency *see* consistency
incubator theories, 11-13, 50, 105-106
indirect instructions, 76
individualists, 15, 49-64
    "hunch" factor, 62-63
    non-team playing, 56-58
    rebellious urge, 49-53
    team development, 59-63
    trust, 53-56
inferiority complexes, 37-38
information gathering, 41, 95
    rule-breaking, 33-34
inherited characteristics, 11-13, 50, 105-106
innovators, 15, 17-28
    incongruities search, 18-21
    salesmanship, 23-25
    types, 26-28
insecurity, 22, 30, 37, 51-52
"intrapreneurialism," 88
inventors, 18

inventrepreneurs, 13, *14*

Laker, Freddy, 34
leadership, 83-84
    unreliable, 87-89
    *see also* team management
Letraset, 20-21
leverage, 46-47
"lieutenants," 91-92
"locus of control," 12, 50
loyalty, 77, 84-86

McDonald's hamburger chain, 17
McKinsey Strategic Management Consultancy, 34
man management, *see* team management
management structure, *66-67*, 69
managers, 15, 65-82
    change of style, 81-82
    entrepreneur and bureaucrat compared, 65-71, *66-67*
    unconventional, 72-73, 78-79
    *see also* team management
marriages, 101-102
mismatches, and innovation, 19, 20
mistrust, 53-56
moderation of style, 61
money, pursuit of, 26, 55, 96-101
mood changes, 86-97

"Napoleon factor," 83-89
NASA, teamwork example, 56
nepostism, 102-104
new products, 19, 20-21
    launching, 42-43
non-planning, 73-74
non-team playing, 56-59
nurturing qualities, 12

observation, 39-41
"obsessive" attitudes, 22
optimism, 12, 25
organizational awareness, 12, 59-60
"other world" syndrome, 52-53

packaging, "hunch" example, 63
partnerships, 89-91
people judgments, 60
persuasion *see* salesmanship
physical activity, 95

planning, 23-24, 73-74
power, pursuit of, 96-102
"prima donnas," 15, 83-104
    colleagues, 91-94
    family relations, 101-104
    "Napoleon factor," 83-89
    partnerships, 89-91
    wealth and power, 96-102
    work capacity, 94-96
professionals, and entrepreneurs, 58
profit orientation, 12
property tycoon, workaholic example, 96
prospectuses, 23-24

reading, 95
"rebellious urge," 49-53
recluses, 54
recognition, 30-31, 51, 100
recruitment, of management staff, 60, 75-77
reliability of behavior *see* constancy
resource commitment and control, *66-67*, 68-69
respectability, 36-37
reward orientation, 12
    *see also* recognition, wealth
risk profile, 43-44
risk-reward ratios, 44-46
risk-taking, 13, 14, 29-48
    competitive urge, 29-31
    concert parties, 34-36
    conduct, 36-37
    failure, 31-32
    risk assessment, 38-48, *46*
    rule-breaking, 33-34
rivalry, 29-31, 53-54
robot, unreliability example, 40

Rothschild family, 33
rule-breaking, 33-34, 78-80
ruthlessness, 77, 99-100

salesmanship, 23-25
seizing opportunities, 66-67, 68
selection of managers, 60, 75-76
self-esteeem *see* insecurity
self-knowledge, 84, 108
self-management, 60-61, 81
software house, ethics example, 80
Stevenson, Howard, 65, 111

strategic vision, 66-67, 68
"strivers," 27
success *see* achievement; applause-seeking; failure
Suez canal, 21
superiority feelings, 30
supermarkets, mismatch example, 19-20
suppliers, 100

talent recognition, 107
team management, 75-78
    and corporate entrepreneurs, 92
    development, 59-62
    importance, 42, 56-59, 57
    recruitment, 60, 74-75
technology applications, 19, 21
television, 21
temper, uncertain, 86-87
temper, unreliability, 86-87
"tendencies," entrepreneurial, 13, *14*, 15, 107-108
test launches, 43
thoroughness, 108
time management, 61
translation service, concert party example, 34-36
trust, 53-56
"trusted lieutenants," 91-92
tunnel vision, 22

unconventional management, 72-73, 78-79
United States, attitude toward failure, 31
unreliable leadership *see* consistency
used car lots, "hunch" example, 62

"visionaries," 26, 94
Vries, Manfred Kets de, 29-30, 49, 112

"watershed decision points," 71
wealth, pursuit of, 26, 55, 96-101
wives, 101-102
work capacity, 12, 13
    workaholics, 94-96